United States
National Interests
in a Changing
World

Donald E. Nuechterlein

United States National Interests in a Changing World

The University Press of Kentucky

ISBN: 0-8131-1287-7

Library of Congress Catalog Card Number: 73-77255

Copyright © 1973 by The University Press of Kentucky

A statewide cooperative scholarly publishing agency
serving Berea College, Centre College of Kentucky,
Eastern Kentucky University, Georgetown College,
Kentucky Historical Society, Kentucky State University,
Morehead State University, Murray State University,
Northern Kentucky State College, Transylvania University,
University of Kentucky, University of Louisville, and
Western Kentucky University.

Editorial and Sales Offices: Lexington, Kentucky 40506

To *Millie and Jonathan*

CONTENTS

PREFACE

THE PURPOSE of this study is to provide policy-makers, scholars, and serious students of international affairs with a framework for assessing United States national interests in the 1970's – by learning from the experience of the post–World War II era and asking some searching questions about what kind of role the United States wishes to play in the world in the future. The study is concerned with the problem of making foreign policy the handmaiden of national interests, rather than having interests predetermined by past policies and institutional prejudices. It is also concerned with executive-legislative relationships in the determination of United States national interests and the means by which the President's perception of national interests is subjected to checks and balances of Congress without depriving him of the authority to make critical decisions when the nation is threatened with a grave international crisis.

Robert Osgood, in his introduction to *America and the World: From the Truman Doctrine to Vietnam,* wrote: "What are America's vital interests and how should it use its power to support them? This is the fundamental foreign policy question facing the United States after two decades of the Cold War."[1] In December 1970, the State Department issued a report of the findings of several task forces which looked into the question of improving the department's performance in the 1970's. In a section entitled "An Improved Capacity to Assess Interests," the report states: "The first step in creating a stronger capacity to perform these three functions is a clearer identification of United States national interests abroad and of the priority among these interests in order to establish a sounder basis for the formulation of foreign policy and the resolution of issues."[2] Both statements reflect a growing awareness of the need for greater precision in defining the United States' national interests and in distinguishing among the different degrees of interest, or stake, which the United States has in various foreign policy issues it now faces. The fact is that the United States, for all its wealth, is not willing to continue expending so high a proportion of its resources on foreign affairs as it has in the past. This means that costs must be given a far greater role in future assessments of the degree of interest the United States has outside its own territorial limits.

This study assumes that the United States will continue to play a great power role in the future, that it will not return to the isolationism of the past, and that the crisis of conscience which affected a large proportion of Americans in the post–Vietnam period will eventually give way to a mood of greater realism about America's role in the world and its ability to shape the course of history. It is not my purpose here to debate whether American policy in Vietnam was moral or immoral; that issue is best left to philosophers. Rather, I am concerned with finding a better way of defining United States national interests in the future, interests which are compatible with the values and sentiments of the American people – not just American leaders. Finally, I believe that the American system of government is capable of responding to the changing attitudes of the people in foreign affairs, and that it will continue to do so.

In a previous volume, I suggested that the final judgment about whether United States military intervention in Vietnam was a wise policy or not would be decided by the American people and Congress on the basis of the costs involved in that effort.[3] By 1968 it was clear that the costs of the Vietnam intervention were far greater than the American people were prepared to accept and the withdrawal of United States ground forces from that conflict without a military decision was evidence that the American people ultimately decide the outer limits of national interests. Yet, a more important question is whether the value of Vietnam in relation to United States worldwide interests warranted the massive use of American military power and economic resources there. A similar question could be posed for any potential United States intervention elsewhere, in the Middle East, Latin America, or the Indian Ocean area: what is the measure by which the President decides that American interests are so threatened, i.e., that the interest is a vital one, that he must contemplate

[1] (Baltimore, Md., 1970), p. 1.
[2] *Department of State Bulletin* 63, no. 1644 (December 28, 1970): 782.
[3] *Thailand and the Struggle for Southeast Asia* (Ithaca, N.Y., 1965), p. 267.

the possible use of armed force to defend them if all other measures fail? This is a central question of this study.

I am indebted to colleagues at the University of Virginia and at the Federal Executive Institute, as well as friends in government, for their help in sharpening the ideas contained in this volume. The final product, however, is fully my responsibility.

1

The Concept of National Interest

THE TERM *national interest* has long been used by statesmen and scholars to describe the foreign-policy goals of nation-states. Charles Beard, in *The Idea of National Interest,* traced the evolution of the phrase from the first nation-states down to the twentieth century and described the historical interests of the United States in essentially economic terms. Walter Lippmann, in *U.S. Foreign Policy: Shield of the Republic,* sought to define United States defense interests in the post–World War II period, drawing on the isolationist experience of the interwar period.

Although the concept of national interest is not new, there has long been considerable ambiguity about its meaning, and most scholars have chosen their own descriptions rather than formulations offered by others. Today the student of international relations finds numerous definitions of national interest, most of which are not conducive to precision in the making of foreign policy. Before attempting a more adequate definition, however, it is well to review briefly what the principal American writers on United States foreign policy have said about the nature and roots of the nation's interests, particularly after the United States became a great power early in this century.

Writing in the 1930's, Beard was principally concerned with what might be called the national economic interest. He argued that the founding fathers, particularly Washington and Hamilton, had a clear perception of what their new nation's interests had to be in order to survive: self-interest rather than sentiment, and a deep appreciation of the limited means available to carry out its policies. Beard believed that the basic national interest of the United States during the first hundred years of its history was an economic interest and that the two major political parties in the country sought to define this economic interest to suit their own purposes. The commercial groups in the East were primarily interested in overseas trade and opposed to westward expansion of the nation across a vast continent. The landed gentry of the South and West, however, favored adding new lands in the West in order to build the political influence of farmers and reduce the power of the Eastern commercial groups. Hamilton and Jefferson were the initial spokesmen of these two forces, which dominated American politics until the Civil War, and also represented the basic cleavage over what America's role in the world ought to be. Beard points out that the two groups differed also on means for carrying out the nation's foreign policy: Eastern commercial interests favored a strong navy and commercial concessions in foreign countries, even overseas bases; the landed interests, on the other hand, opposed overseas involvements and pressed for the acquisition of new territories from Spain, France, and Mexico – sometimes through treaty and at other times through war. National security was not a principal concern of the United States, except for a brief period during the War of 1812, because no foreign power had the capability of invading the country and forcing it to submit to its will. The Monroe Doctrine was a feasible policy because of the support of the British Navy in the Atlantic. Thus, the new nation's interests could afford to be based on economics rather than on military power.[1]

A different view of what constitutes the basic national interest of the United States was provided in the post–World War II period by Hans Morgenthau, whose ideas were forcefully set forth in his widely read textbook *Politics among Nations*. Both in this volume and in his shorter treatise, *In Defense of the National Interest,* Morgenthau argued that power, primarily industrial and military power, was the means by which nations survived in an essentially competitive world, and that nations which neglected self-interest and national power succumbed to the influence and intimidation of other states which emphasized them. Morgenthau deplored what he termed the "utopian" view of the world held by the "idealists" and favored instead a "realistic" outlook based on national self-interest. Like Charles Beard, he argued that the realism of the founding fathers had made it possible

1 Charles A. Beard, *The Idea of National Interest* (Chicago, 1934).

for the new nation to chart a wise policy which avoided entanglements with the great powers of Europe and permitted American commerce to prosper. The difficulties which the United States encountered in its international relations in the twentieth century, he asserted, resulted from the moralism and utopianism of leaders such as Woodrow Wilson; they subordinated the self-interest of the United States to universal principles which often were unattainable and therefore proved deeply frustrating to the nation.[2] Morgenthau's view was summed up in an article entitled "Another Great Debate: The National Interest of the United States" in which he argued:

> The contest between utopianism and realism is not tantamount to a contest between principle and expediency, morality and immorality, although some spokesmen for the former would like to have it that way. The contest is rather between one type of political morality and another type of political morality, one taking as its standard universal moral principles abstractly formulated, the other weighing these principles against the moral requirements of concrete political action, their relative merits to be decided by a prudent evaluation of the political consequences to which they are likely to lead.[3]

George Kennan, a professional diplomat turned scholar, shared Morgenthau's view of the world and the need for realistic thinking as the basis of foreign-policy formulation. He too criticized the utopianism of those who shared Wilson's outlook because such views, he argued, led to serious errors in judgment about the real nature of international politics and of the best way for the United States to advance its basic national interests. Both Morgenthau and Kennan were strong advocates of the balance-of-power principle of international relations, in which great powers seek to maintain international stability and relative peace through the balancing of military and economic power, and in which no one nation could become so powerful as to threaten the security of others. Kennan also became associated with the so-called elitist view of foreign policy-making, arguing that the general public neither appreciated nor cared about the intricacies of foreign affairs and that skilled statesmen and diplo-

---

[2] Hans J. Morgenthau, *In Defense of the National Interest* (New York, 1951).
[3] *American Political Science Review* 46, no. 4 (December 1952): 961–88.

mats should be given great latitude in determining national interests and the policies most likely to advance them.[4]

The theologian-scholar Reinhold Niebuhr, who began publishing his ideas on the nature of the world in the pre–World War II period and continued to have considerable influence in the postwar period, was interested in finding a place for both idealism and realism in the formulation of United States national interests. Niebuhr was deeply disturbed, as were many of his contemporaries, by the shattering impact of World War I on the world order and on the idealism that had characterized the intellectual community. *Moral Man and Immoral Society,* published in 1932, reflected a new sense of realism in his thinking about the behavior of states in the international community; in it Niebuhr reluctantly concluded that the role of power could not be ignored as one of the major elements controlling the relations of states. In 1953, his widely read volume entitled *The Irony of American History* elaborated the view that both moral values and power must be considered in the formulation of national interests and in the pursuit of international peace.[5] Or, as Ernest Lefever observed in *Ethics and United States Foreign Policy*: "Power politics and ethics are often thought of as mutually exclusive and morally incompatible poles or political alternatives. The writer believes there is no foreign policy, however noble, which does not include power politics, or however cynical, which does not include moral considerations."[6]

Perhaps the most thorough research on the subject of United States national interests in this century was conducted by Robert Osgood, whose comprehensive volume *Ideals and Self-Interest in America's Foreign Relations* was published in 1953. Osgood's view was that egoism and idealism had been competing concepts in determining United States foreign policy since the turn of the twentieth century, when the acquisition of the Philippines in the Pacific and of Cuba in the Caribbean resulted in an imperialistic trend in United States foreign policy; the most notable proponents of this viewpoint were Theodore Roosevelt and Al-

4 George F. Kennan, *American Diplomacy, 1900–1950* (Chicago, 1951).
5 See also Niebuhr's *Structure of Nations and Empires* (New York, 1959).
6 (New York, 1957), p. 4.

fred T. Mahan. Osgood examined how the two distinct viewpoints – egoism and idealism – developed into two competing foreign policies, with the Republican party adopting the former and the Democrats tending toward the latter. Osgood defined the two points of view as follows: "National self-interest is understood to mean a state of affairs valued solely for its benefit to the nation . . . . An ideal is a standard of conduct or a state of affairs worthy of achievement by virtue of its universal moral value."[7] He went on to argue that nations, like individuals, seldom act out of either purely selfish motives or pure idealism, that most actions and policies are a blending of the two. The degree to which a nation acts out of self-interest or idealistic motives is the key to discovering the basis of its national interest, he concluded.

Another scholar who wrote extensively in the postwar period on national interest and foreign policy was Arnold Wolfers, one of a group of writers who sought to bridge the gap between the idealists and the realists. Wolfers noted that the term *national interest* had become, in the post–World War II period, practically synonymous with a formula for national security and that, unless explicitly denied, those who stress national interest as the basis of foreign policy may be assumed to mean that "priority shall be given to measures of security." Wolfers believed there was a preoccupation among scholars and statesmen with national security and military power, which he viewed as not surprising during the 1950's when there was a major emphasis in the United States on building up strategic military power; but, he argued, one did not have to be obsessed with national security in order to be realistic about the goals and interests of the United States in the world.[8]

The trend in the 1950's to associate national interest primarily with national security was unfortunate because it gave a distorted view of what national interests consist of and made it more difficult to use the term in a broader context, namely, the pursuit of goals in the international environment which the nation is generally agreed upon during a particular time frame. This

---

7 (Chicago, 1953), p. 4.
8 "National Security as an Ambiguous Symbol," *Political Science Quarterly* 67, no. 4 (December 1952): 481–502.

view of national interest was described by Paul Seabury in his book *Power, Freedom, and Diplomacy*: "We might thus conceive of the national interest as a kaleidoscopic process by which forces latent in American society seek to express certain political and economic aspirations in world politics through the highest organs of state. To comprehend this process, we must not merely understand something of the formal governmental processes by which foreign policy is made, but also penetrate into the depth of the nation itself to discern the wellsprings of thought, ideology, and smaller interests that feed into the mainstreams of American policy abroad."[9]

From this brief review of some of the principal writings on the subject of national interest, it is apparent that there is no general agreement among scholars on how to define the term or what policies should flow from its definition. In fact, there is no common conceptual framework in which serious discussion can take place. It is desirable, therefore, that this study of American national interests begin with an effort to provide such a framework, for if we can be more precise about definition, especially about degrees of interest that should guide policy formulation, we may find greater utility in the term *national interest* than has been the case during the past thirty years.

DEFINITIONS: NATIONAL INTEREST, PUBLIC INTEREST, STRATEGIC INTEREST, AND PRIVATE INTEREST

For purposes of definition, it is well to draw a distinction between the terms *national interest* and *public interest*. The *public interest* may be viewed as the well-being of the American people and American enterprise within the territorial boundaries of the United States. The *national interest,* on the other hand, refers to the well-being of American citizens and American enterprise involved in international relations and affected by political forces beyond the administrative control of the United States government. This is especially important when the rights of Americans are endangered by the policies of other nations which are antagonistic to those of the United States. Obviously, the public

[9] (New York, 1963), p. 87.

interest and the national interest are not mutually exclusive: indeed, the public interest is heavily influenced by the nature of the international environment in which the United States interacts, particularly when there is a threat of war; similarly, the national interest is influenced by the degree of social stability and political unity prevailing within the country at any given time. For purposes of this discussion, it is useful to think of the public interest as being the concern of federal, state, and local government – with the President sharing his authority with Congress, the courts, and the fifty states – and the national interest being the concern only of the federal government, with the President, rather than Congress or the courts, exercising the principal authority and responsibility for the nation's welfare.[10]

Strategic interests are a second-order interest and derive from a clear perception of national interests. They are concerned with the political, economic, and military means of protecting the nation against military dangers and are defined to a large degree by geography, the availability of scarce resources, military technology, and the limitation of damage which could be inflicted on American territory or that of an ally. Occasionally, strategic interests tend to determine national interests, rather than the reverse, and in such cases confusion and overemphasis on military security often results.

Private interests, on the other hand, refer to the activities of United States citizens and companies abroad whose prosperity does not affect the security or economic well-being of the entire United States.

BASIC NATIONAL INTERESTS

The United States, like most nations, has both changing and unchanging national interests, some of which it has pursued consistently – although with varying degrees of intensity – over long periods of time, and some of which it has pursued for

---

10 The President's primary role in setting U.S. foreign-policy objectives has been well established by precedent and decisions of the courts (see Edwin Corwin, *The Presidency: Office and Powers* [New York, 1957]). However, the degree of his authority in committing the nation to war without a formal declaration by Congress has been the subject of intense debate in the aftermath of the Vietnam experience. (See Ch. 3.)

short periods and then altered because of changing world conditions or domestic political considerations. In the 1970's, the United States has three basic, relatively unchanging, national interests: two of them are as old as the Republic itself, and the third is a more recent interest growing out of the experiences of two world wars. All United States interests and policies can be fitted into one of these three broad categories: defense, trade and commerce, and the building of a stable world order.[11] These long-term interests may be defined as follows:

1. *Defense:* Protection of the people, territory, and institutions of the United States against potential foreign dangers. This is usually referred to as the national defense interest and it has been pursued with varying intensity throughout American history, as the government and the people have perceived foreign dangers arising and threatening the security of the nation.

2. *Economic:* Promotion of United States international trade and investment, including protection of United States private interests in foreign countries. This may be called the national economic interest. It has been historically the most important national interest of this country because geography made it possible for the new nation to concentrate its energies on trade rather than defense during most of its history.

3. *World order:* Establishment of a peaceful international environment in which disputes between nations can be resolved without resort to war and in which collective security rather than unilateral action is employed to deter or cope with aggression. This is sometimes referred to as the international interest, and it came to prominence after the United States achieved great power status early in the twentieth century when the idealism of the American people began to exert influence on the formula-

[11] Some may argue that the United States has a fourth basic national interest, namely, an ideological interest which includes promoting American democracy and the free enterprise system abroad. While I agree that there is some validity in this view, I am inclined to believe that promoting American democracy is a part of building a stable world order and that promoting the free enterprise system is a part of the national economic interest.

tion of foreign policy. This basic interest is primarily concerned with the establishment of a stable world order in which peaceful change can be managed by the great powers and potential aggressors deterred. This interest is also concerned with questions of alliance systems and balance of power.[12]

In the post–World War II period, the United States pursued all three of these basic interests, but national defense received greater attention and national resources than did the others from 1950 until about 1970. In the early postwar years, 1945–1948, idealism and optimism were characteristic of the American public mood, and economic interests and world-order interests, i.e., building a better and more peaceful world, dominated United States foreign policy. However, by the late 1940's, particularly after the Communist coup in Czechoslovakia in 1948 and the Red Army's conquest of China in 1949, the mood of the nation changed to one of disillusionment and pessimism. National defense then was perceived as the most important basic interest of the country, and this was reflected in the rapid build-up of the armed forces and in the sharp increases in defense expenditures following the outbreak of war in Korea in 1950. For the next twenty years, national defense dominated the thinking of most foreign policy-makers, and the efforts at arms limitation and support for international organizations occupied a lesser role in the shaping of United States policies. Beginning about 1968, however, the mood of the country shifted again and the American people gave more emphasis to domestic needs and priorities as they became disillusioned over the government's inability to solve the war in Indo-China. The detente policies of the Nixon administration received, therefore, wide approbation, as exhibited in the 1972 presidential election.

The problem of correctly defining national interests lies not so much in identifying the broad unchanging interests, but rather in assessing the intensity of the interest – or stake – at different moments in history and the propensity of the government to use pressure, including armed force, to defend or enhance certain national interests in preference to others, and at the expense of

---

[12] For a detailed discussion of the concepts of collective security and world order, see Inis L. Claude, Jr., *Power and International Relations* (New York, 1962).

other nations. For example, the United States has long had an interest in freedom of the seas for both economic and defense reasons, but the willingness of the government to use military force to protect that interest has changed over time, as its perception of its defense and economic interests has altered. United States policy following the seizure of the navy ship *Pueblo* by North Korea early in 1968 is a case in point.

In sum, we are concerned with the degree of interest the United States feels in specific issues relating to its three basic national interests, and with the basis for determining which threats are so important to its defense, economic, or world-order interests that it would contemplate the use of armed force to protect them against encroachment by a foreign power. It is the intensity of concern about any of the three basic interests at a given period of time which forms the basis of policy-making in foreign affairs. These intensities or degrees of interest constitute a different category which we will call "transitory" because they are subject to change depending on the government's perception of their urgency at any given time.

TRANSITORY INTERESTS

The term *transitory*, as used here, does not imply that an interest is present at one period of time and not at another; rather, it suggests that certain specific issues falling under any of the three basic interests described above may receive more attention from policy-makers at some times than at others. The degree of interest involved usually depends on the President's perception of the international environment within which the United States conducts foreign policy and on his perception of the political climate in the United States. Looking at transitory or short-term interests in this light, it is possible to visualize a four-tiered scale of priorities as a basis for defining more precisely the amount of value the nation, acting through its government, attaches to specific foreign-policy issues. This scale of priorities may be defined as follows: (1) *survival* interests, where the very existence of the nation is in peril; (2) *vital* interests, where probable serious harm could result to the security and well-being of the nation if strong measures, including the use of force, are not taken by the government; (3) *major* interests, where potential serious harm could come to the nation if no action is taken to counter an unfavorable trend abroad; and (4) *peripheral,* or minor, interests, where little if any harm will result to the entire nation if a "wait and see" policy is adopted.[13]

Survival interests: The primary interest of any nation-state, the *sine qua non* of its existence, is the protection of its citizens and their institutions against attack by foreign enemies. A government which cannot provide protection for its people, either through its own resources or in alliance with other nations, probably will not survive for long. Therefore, defense against the threat of an imminent enemy attack must be considered as a survival interest of any power that hopes to maintain its independence in the international environment. The major difference between a survival interest and a vital interest, in this scale of priorities, lies both in the nature of and the imminence of a military threat to the nation. An ultimatum issued by a major power to its neighbor to concede territory or face invasion is a survival interest to the country receiving the ultimatum, as was the case with Poland in 1939. Subversion and insurgency, on the other hand, would not usually constitute a survival interest to the nation under pressure because it would have time to take measures to deal with the insurgency before it reached the stage where survival might be at stake. South Vietnam in 1961 was in this situation, although by 1965 the internal situation had deteriorated to such an extent that the collapse of the state was probable without foreign military help.

The United States alone, of all the major powers which entered World War II, did not have its survival interests threatened, although President Roosevelt and other leaders perceived that if Germany and Japan emerged victorious from the war the political and economic institutions of the United States might be

---

[13] The assumption is made that the United States, as a global power, would find it difficult to assume a posture of no interest in any part of the world, in outer space, or on the ocean floor. Therefore, the term *peripheral interest* as used here includes all those local problems and issues which do not seriously concern policy-makers because the outcome is not likely to affect any important United States interests.

sharply altered and the security of the country directly endangered. The attack on Pearl Harbor did not in itself constitute a survival threat to the country, as there was little possibility at that time of an invasion of the mainland or the overthrow of the nation's leadership. All other powers of the prewar period – Britain, France, the U.S.S.R., Germany, Italy, Japan, and China – were either invaded by enemy forces or threatened with invasion. For all of them, the war constituted a survival interest because losing the war clearly meant occupation by enemy forces and a complete change in the political life of the nation. Smaller powers, unlike major powers, often do not resist a powerful neighbor when their survival interests are at stake because they may conclude that the cost of resistance is higher than the cost of submission. Denmark and Thailand are examples of states which submitted to German and Japanese threats during World War II because they concluded that survival was more likely if the nations were occupied rather than destroyed by invaders. Larger powers more often believe that resistance to invasion is in their national interest.

If we define survival interest as an imminent danger of invasion or of massive aerial attack on the homeland of a country, we would have to conclude that the United States has not had its survival interests threatened since the War of 1812, when the British invaded Washington, D. C.; the Civil War might have been in this category if a European power, the British for example, had intervened in the struggle. Neither World War I nor World War II would be considered a survival interest of the United States by this definition, although potentially the survival of the nation might have been endangered if Germany and Japan had dominated Europe and Asia. Both wars were fought by the United States because vital, not survival, interests were threatened. (Nevertheless, Roosevelt mobilized the nation and fought in World War II in a way that would lead one to conclude that survival interests were at stake.) The only episode in the post–World War II period when a United States survival interest might have been in question was the Cuban Missile Crisis of 1962, when the Soviet Union sought to place medium-range missiles with nuclear warheads in Cuba.[14] President Kennedy decided that if he did nothing in the face of so bold an attempt to upset the balance of power in North America the credibility of the United States nuclear deterrent – upon which the defense of the non-Communist world depended – would have been questioned to such an extent that survival of the United States as a world power could have been placed in doubt. Therefore, the President followed policies in that crisis which clearly demonstrated his intention to risk war with the Soviet Union, if necessary, to remove the threat from Cuba.

Thus far we have discussed survival interest strictly in terms of national defense – one of the basic, unchanging, interests described above. Another aspect of national defense has been given increased attention during the last decade. This is the growing conviction, both in the United States and in the Soviet Union, that the survival of both countries may be imperiled by a continuation of the nuclear arms race and that means must be found to limit both the number of countries possessing nuclear weapons and the number of nuclear weapons possessed by the two superpowers. The prevention of nuclear war is clearly a survival interest because nuclear destruction of the United States would make it unlikely that the American system of government could survive, even though a segment of its population might. Therefore, the United States has found itself in the paradoxical position since World War II of being at the zenith of its power and influence and also for the first time in a century and a half, of having its national survival threatened by intercontinental missiles. Geography, although still a favorable factor insofar as protection against conventional warfare is concerned, no longer makes this country immune from massive destruction; this fact has produced profound changes in Americans' perception of the country's national interests, particularly among the generation that has grown up since 1945.

Because the prevention of nuclear war between the United

[14] One might argue that the survival of the U.S. was not actually in question because in the deployment of these missiles, the Soviets gave no evidence of intention to use them for any purpose other than political pressures on the U.S. and Latin American countries.

States and the Soviet Union has come to be considered a matter of survival interest, both countries have made serious efforts since 1963 to reach an understanding on this critical question. The Nuclear Test Ban Treaty of 1963 between the United States and the Soviet Union was a momentous first step along the road to international agreement to control the use of nuclear weapons. Similarly, the Limited Nuclear Non-proliferation Treaty of 1967, ratified by over one hundred nations, raised hopes that non-nuclear nations will refrain from developing these weapons and thus facilitate international efforts to work out other agreements for the limitation of armaments. The Strategic Arms Limitation Talks (SALT) which began in Helsinki in 1969 and culminated in the Moscow Accords of May 1972 between the United States and the Soviet Union are thus a matter of survival interest to both powers because failure to reach agreement could involve them in another round of strategic weapons escalation, thus adding to international tensions and a greater likelihood of nuclear confrontation. Implicit in these negotiations, which will continue and include discussions of limiting conventional weapons, is an understanding by the superpowers that national survival is more important than most political issues that divide them at present – both in regard to their national interests and also their ideological beliefs. No other power comes near these two in present or even potential capability to inflict nuclear destruction on the world; that is why agreement between the United States and the Soviet Union on the limitation of armaments – particularly nuclear arms – is crucial to the survival interests of all countries.

Vital interests: The vital interests of the United States are the protection of the country against probable dangers to its political survival and economic well-being and the promotion of a peaceful international environment. Vital interests differ from survival interests primarily in the matter of time – the urgency with which decisions must be made to deal with an international crisis which could threaten the nation's survival. The decisions President Kennedy made in October 1962 after Soviet missiles were discovered in Cuba had greater urgency, for example, than did those of President Truman in 1950 when North Korea invaded

South Korea or, similarly, when President Johnson in 1965 decided to send combat forces to South Vietnam. The periodic crises arising over the status of Berlin were also in a different category from that of Cuba in 1962 because, although these were serious situations which could have triggered a war in Europe, they had been anticipated and contingency planning had been in progress. Furthermore, the safety of American soil was not at issue, as was perceived to be the case in the Cuban crisis. Most international crises with which the United States has had to deal in the post–World War II period were perceived as vital, not survival, interests: for example, the Berlin Blockade, the Korean War, the Taiwan Straits Crisis, Lebanon, Congo, Dominican Republic, and Vietnam.

Some critics may argue that the difference between survival and vital interests is artificial because the term *vital* means life-giving and therefore should be accorded the highest priority of value. The view held here, however, is that although both terms – *vital* and *survival* – have to do with the life of the nation, one deals with imminent danger of death while the other is only potentially fatal. An analogy may be made to one victim who is threatened with a pistol in his head, and another who is threatened with a blunt instrument. Both may die from the wounds inflicted if the threats are carried out, but the chances for survival are much lower in the former case.

In the crises noted above, where United States vital interests were thought to be at stake, all of them involved the survival interests of the country directly affected, with the possible exception of the Dominican Republic. In Berlin, the existence of a non-Communist West Germany – and perhaps of Italy and France as well – was thought to be at stake when Stalin closed the border in 1948. In Korea, the Republic of China, Lebanon, Congo, and Vietnam, the independence of these states was clearly in question and the United States had to decide whether their conquest by hostile forces would seriously affect United States interests, or affect them only moderately in the short term. Thus, one of the important ingredients in determining a vital interest is the assessment of how important another nation's survival interest is to the United States.

Broadly speaking, there are four matters of vital interest to the United States: (1) maintaining a strategic balance of power with the Soviet Union; (2) assisting those nations allied with the United States to defend themselves; (3) promoting a strong United States economy with access to world markets and resources; and (4) building world peace through negotiations with major antagonists – principally the Soviet Union and Communist China. These four interests may not be mutually compatible, and the task of policy-making is deciding which are more important at what times, and under what circumstances.

Clearly, the maintenance of a strategic balance of world power between the United States and the Soviet Union is a vital interest of the United States, probably its most important vital interest. The assumption of American foreign policy after World War II was that if the United States is superior in strength to any other power, the danger of war will be lessened. Therefore, nuclear deterrence, based on United States superiority in nuclear weapons and delivery capability, was a hallmark of American policy. Even when the Soviet Union developed intercontinental missiles and acquired the capability of inflicting large destruction on the United States, the strategy of deterrence was valid so long as the United States had a second-strike capability – which assumed sufficiency in protected ICBM's and other delivery systems, such as Polaris submarines. The debate over ABM systems and multiple warhead missiles is part of the critical problem of the strategic balance of power; the assumption made by most United States leaders is that if the Soviet Union were to gain a strategic advantage over the United States, it would use that advantage to threaten United States vital interests in other parts of the world.[15]

If it is easy to agree that maintenance of a strategic balance of power with the Soviet Union is a vital interest, the second priority – assistance to allies to resist aggression from Communist powers – is open to much dispute. The differences arise out of definition of the words *aggression* and *communist*, and the importance of allies.

In the post–World War II period, when the United States

[15] Chairman Khrushchev's threatening words to President Kennedy in June 1961 concerning Berlin is an example of this viewpoint.

abandoned its prewar isolationist policy and made defense alliances with many nations in Europe, Asia, and Latin America, it was clear that the enemy against which the treaties were made was the Soviet Union in Europe and the Middle East, and Communist China, North Korea, and North Vietnam in Asia. In fact, the United States appended a protocol to the Manila Pact which obligated it to defend the treaty area only against Communist aggression. But this did not answer the question whether internal subversion and insurgency, as in Vietnam and Laos, were the same as Communist aggression across borders. In Europe in the early 1950's, the threat was clearly a military one posed by the Soviet troops crossing the borders of Germany. (The possibility of an internal Communist takeover in Italy and France had diminished before the North Atlantic Pact was signed in 1949.) In Southeast Asia, however, the threat was subversion and insurgency, not a conventional attack over a border. Yet, to many Americans, the two forms of aggression were inseparable. Again, the terms of the Manila Pact drew a distinction between overt aggression, which would be met by the signatories in accordance with their constitutional processes, and indirect aggression, which required signatories only to discuss what should be done.[16]

The answer to what is the United States interest when an ally is threatened by overt attack, however, is not in doubt; this is clearly a vital interest because, as Secretary of State Dean Rusk so often pointed out, the credibility of the United States' word is dependent on whether it will honor its commitments. Both the North Atlantic Pact and the Manila Pact were carefully debated by Congress, and it was the clear consensus that defense of the signatory nations was a vital interest of the United States.[17] It is therefore reasonable to conclude that when the United States enters into a defense treaty with other countries, when Congress has clearly assented to the commitment in accordance with its constitutional role to "advise and consent" to foreign treaties,

[16] Southeast Asia Collective Defense Treaty, Article IV.

[17] Arguments that the wording of the Manila Pact leaves much more room for interpretation than does the North Atlantic Pact are not valid; the clear implication of both treaties is that the U.S. is obligated to act in case of attack, even though the Manila treaty takes account of the constitutional right of Congress to commit American forces to war.

this is confirmation that a vital interest of the United States has been decided. This should not preclude, however, a periodic review of these commitments, to determine whether they should continue to be vital interests in light of changing international conditions.

The United States was so concerned with defense interests in the 1950's and 1960's that it sometimes lost sight of another vital interest, namely, a strong economy having access to world markets, and a strong currency to sustain its economic position in the world. This factor is well understood by economists and bankers but received less public attention in the 1950's and 1960's than defense interests. Nevertheless, the international economic system has been developed to such a degree of interdependence among the non-Communist nations that an economic failure by any key nation in the system sharply affects all others. The pressure on the pound sterling in the 1960's caused Britain to curtail overseas deployments of troops. More recently, the serious balance-of-payments problems encountered by the United States in the late 1960's and early 1970's led to President Nixon's sudden decision in August 1971 to impose a surtax on imports, untie the dollar from a fixed gold price, and institute wage and price controls on the United States economy. The disastrous political consequences that flowed from the stock market crash of 1929 illustrated the importance of a strong international economic system to the maintenance of world political stability. Economic warfare among nations has been a cause of political strife in the past; it is of vital interest to the United States to support an international economic system in which all nations, including the United States, have an opportunity to increase their trade and improve their standard of living and thus reduce international tensions and risks of war. However, as the President's actions in 1971 showed, the economic well-being of the United States will not be subordinated to this international goal.

A fourth area of vital interest to the United States is enhancement of the peaceful resolution of conflict with other powers through negotiations. The realist school would argue that conflict is inevitable in international relations and that the best way to deal with it is for a nation to build up sufficient power to insure that no others will challenge it successfully on any matter of vital interest. But many thoughtful persons of the idealist school believe that such a cynical view of the world will lead ultimately to war, either through miscalculation or because a local conflict may escalate to large war. The Arab-Israeli conflict in 1967 and the Berlin Crisis in 1961 are examples of international disputes that could have involved the Soviet Union and the United States in war had efforts not been made to contain them. The confrontation over Vietnam in the 1960's contained a similar risk, although the danger of a larger war diminished significantly after 1968, and particularly after President Nixon's visit to China in 1972.

The important consideration here is that the threat of nuclear warfare makes it dangerous for the superpowers to engage in competition for power and influence without also making efforts to reach understandings on the limits of their competition. This is not to say that either power feels any less antipathy for the political system embraced by the other, or that it would not take advantage of any weakness shown by the other in pursuing its interests. However, the development of nuclear weapons has so changed the implications of warfare between these great powers that, in their own self-interest, they have found it expedient to discuss ways of "de-fusing" the Vietnam war, the Arab-Israeli conflict, and the Berlin issue. *Accommodation* is probably too strong a word to describe efforts of the Soviet Union and the United States to find the means of avoiding confrontations over each other's vital interests, yet, American behavior when Soviet troops went into Czechoslovakia in 1968 was an example of restraint, as was Soviet behavior when the United States sent troops to quell a revolution in the Dominican Republic in 1965. Unquestionably, the Soviet Union's concern over its relations with China since the mid-1960's has contributed to its willingness to discuss ways of improving relations with the United States. Similarly, the United States has an interest in seeking Soviet help in reducing the risks of war in the Middle East, and it also has an important interest, probably a vital interest, in avoiding conflict with the People's Republic of China and, perhaps, in helping her to resist Soviet pressures. In 1972, this policy seemed to be well on its way to fruition after Peking was admitted to the United Nations and President Nixon made his historic visit to China. Although the degree of rapprochement between Washington and Peking was the subject of intense speculation in 1972, there was little doubt that the United States and China had parallel interests in reaching a detente, because of the growing power of the Soviet Union in Central Asia and Japan's dynamic growth as an economic power in East Asia. The President's visit, even though diplomatic relations were not immediately established, went far toward giving China the great power status it desires and has had a beneficial effect on promoting peace in East Asia. Japanese Prime Minister Tanaka's visit to Peking in September 1972 reinforced this favorable trend.[18]

In addition to these two large Communist powers, which were openly antagonistic to American interests in the 1950's and 1960's, a word should also be said about nations whose interests are potentially in conflict with the United States' vital interests. Germany, Japan, and France are major world powers today whose interests are not necessarily consonant with those of the United States, and yet, it is a vital interest to all of them to make serious efforts to insure that differences in their interests do not endanger the good relations which have existed between them and the United States in the post–World War II period. Of the three, France has shown greater evidence of independent action in foreign affairs than the others; this was shown already in the early postwar period when France suffered from a defeatist complex, growing out of the German occupation of the war years and France's inability to hold her colonies in Southeast Asia. A serious blow was dealt to France when the United States refused to support the French (as well as British and Israeli) invasion of Egypt in 1956 and forced a humiliating withdrawal of its forces. When General DeGaulle came to power in 1958, he opposed United States interests in Europe and elsewhere, and favored greater reliance on French arms and diplomacy. Even after De-Gaulle retired in 1968, his successors followed an independent policy in the Middle East by agreeing to sell jets to Libya at a

[18] The effects of the Washington-Peking detente on the balance of power in Asia are discussed in Ch. 7.

time when the United States was seeking to avoid an arms race in that area. France's efforts to use the European Common Market to challenge United States economic interests in Europe continued even after it agreed in 1972 to let Britain, Denmark and Ireland join the organization.

United States and German interests, on the other hand, remained convergent over the years, despite some differences over economic policy, because the Bonn government needed American support in negotiating with the Soviet Union and Eastern Europe. But eventually American forces in Germany will be greatly reduced – because of domestic pressures in the United States – and Germany will have to rely more on itself. It will continue to be a vital interest of the United States to maintain close relations with Germany in order to influence Soviet policy in Europe; but it is also important for the United States to preserve good relations between Bonn and its neighbors in order to encourage stability in Europe. By 1972, Europe had made steady progress toward economic unity, although similar success in the political realm seemed to be some distance in the future.

Japan poses no current threat to United States defense interests in the Pacific, but it would be foolish to assume that Japanese and United States interests will be harmonious. It is a vital interest of the United States to seek ways to accommodate the interests of Japan so that future differences do not result in another conflict of interests such as developed in the late 1930's. It is probably only a matter of time until Japan again becomes a naval power in the Pacific, and perhaps an air power as well. As the United States reduces its own involvement in Southeast Asia, Japan's political role inevitably will grow – just as its economic role has already become paramount there and in Australia. Therefore, it is a vital American interest to find ways to make its long-term interests in the Pacific consonant with those of Japan. The concession which President Nixon made to the Japanese government over Okinawa in 1969 was an effort to insure continued partnership with this dynamic nation. The question is not whether it is a vital United States interest to seek such an accommodation of national interests with Japan, but how far the United States is willing to go in granting Japan economic and military concessions. By 1972 this seemed less likely than before.[19]

A final word should be said concerning the difference between vital and survival interests; this has to do with the means to be employed in dealing with threats to those interests. In the case of a survival interest, i.e., a threat of invasion or a nuclear attack, all the means available to a President will be used to defend the nation, and little debate will take place in Congress or the public about its appropriateness. This is because in matters of survival interest, and in some cases of vital interest such as World War II, the Constitution gives the President, as Commander-in-Chief, wide powers to deal with a national emergency. In matters of vital interest, however – cases where the danger is not perceived as imminent – there usually is some difference of view in the country over what is an appropriate response to such a danger. In such cases – Berlin, Korea, Vietnam – the response is likely to be a limited military action rather than an all-out effort. Thus, President Truman sent troops to defend South Korea, and President Johnson sent troops to prevent a military takeover of South Vietnam, yet both had limited objectives and both avoided enlarging these conflicts by refusing to attack China or the Soviet Union. Had either of these conflicts been considered a survival interest of the United States, Chinese and possibly Soviet territory would not have been off-limits to American bombers.

Major interests: The major interests of the United States are those which potentially could affect the security of the nation, the economic well-being of its people, and the stability of the international system if no actions are taken. Major interests differ from vital and survival interests in the degree of danger perceived, particularly if a security issue is involved, and the amount of time available to find a peaceful solution to the problem. Major United States interests include a threat to the security of an ally when open aggression is not clearly established; a threatened revolution or rebellion within an allied country, when Communist influence and subversion are present; disputes be-

[19] President Nixon's handling of trade relations and exchange-rate negotiations with Japan in 1971 was evidence of a new hard line toward Japan in economic matters.

tween two non-Communist states, when the outcome might adversely affect the balance of power in a given area; a serious threat to large private American investments abroad, particularly if expropriation of property without compensation is the issue; restriction of United States shipping in important international waterways; and a flagrant violation of international law, or threat to United Nations peace-keeping efforts. Major United States interests were involved in the expropriation by Peru of United States oil interests in 1968; the attempted Communist coup d'etat in Indonesia in 1965; the India-Pakistan wars in 1965 and 1971; North Korean efforts to restrict naval use of the Sea of Japan; and the continuing Arab-Israeli conflict. A fundamental difference between a major and a vital interest lies in a nation's perception of the degree of danger involved and the amount of time available to use diplomatic means. In the cases cited above, the President probably would not risk war unless the security of the United States or a key ally was threatened by a great power.[20]

We concluded earlier that when the United States signs a defense treaty with another country after full debate and a two-thirds affirmative vote in the Senate, the protection of that country against armed attack becomes a vital interest of the United States. However, the internal security and economic well-being of that nation is also an important interest, and this should be classified as a major interest. It is particularly true for those allies which fall into the category of developing countries, such as Thailand, the Philippines and Korea. The commitment to defend them in case of attack is evidence of a vital United States interest, but American economic and military assistance, and other policies designed to strengthen them internally, is evidence of a major interest. This is an important distinction, because economic and military assistance is designed to make a country strong enough to defend itself against "wars of national liberation" and other communist pressures, that do not involve an armed attack across a border.

One of the difficult problems a great power encounters in determining the degree of its own interest is a threat to the vital

[20] This seems to be the thrust of the Nixon Doctrine on local wars.

interest of an ally. A dilemma often arises over whether to aid the ally, even when the issue is of only major or peripheral interest to the great power, or deny that support and run the risk of losing the ally's support when needed. A case in point was the Suez Crisis in 1956, when the British and French governments perceived their vital interests to be threatened by Nasser's nationalization of the Suez Canal, and then proceeded to use force in an attempt to crush him. The United States refused to support that venture and even joined the Soviet Union in denouncing what was thought to be a breach of the United Nations Charter; nine years later, when the United States perceived its own vital interests to be at stake in Vietnam, neither Britain nor France provided any military support to the effort in Vietnam, even though both were members of SEATO.[21] Another case in point was Pakistan's disillusionment over United States failure to support her cause against India, when those two nations fought a short war in 1965 over Kashmir.[22] Similarly, Thailand's disappointment over United States policy in Laos in 1961 was caused by American failure to support a Thai vital interest when it did not coincide with its own interest.

The promotion of trade and commerce and economic investment abroad has traditionally been an important United States interest. The great efforts made by the United States, beginning during World War II, to build an international economic system and to promote monetary stability and economic development throughout the world has continued to be a cornerstone of American foreign policy. This policy is based on the assumption that economic development is the key to political stability, and that it is a major, perhaps a vital, interest to provide opportunities for all nations to achieve economic progress through free institutions rather than under a totalitarian system. Hence, the United States gave large-scale economic assistance to Europe and to many developing nations in the postwar period and supported international organizations whose objectives were similar to its own.

---

21 This is not to imply a cause-and-effect relationship between these two episodes but rather to illustrate how differently allies sometimes perceive their own interests, and the policies that flow from that perception.

22 U.S. support for Pakistan when India invaded East Pakistan in December 1971 was in contrast with its hands-off policy in 1965.

Freedom of the seas is an interest that has been important to the United States since the founding of the Republic. Until recently, it was usually considered vital to this country that its ships be permitted to sail anywhere outside a three-mile limit of foreign territory. The War of 1812 was precipitated by this issue, as was the Spanish-American War. The sinking of the *Lusitania* by a German U-boat in 1915 and the resumption of unrestricted submarine warfare in 1917 were key factors in causing the United States to enter World War I. Today, absolute freedom of the seas everywhere is not a vital United States interest; the United States is less willing than previously to respond militarily to the loss of a ship in international waters because the consequences of such action might be too serious. For example, the United States did not retaliate militarily against North Korea when the latter captured the U.S.S. *Pueblo* in 1968, nor when Israel attacked the U.S.S. *Liberty* in 1967. Also, when President Sukarno declared in 1960 that Sunda and Lombak straits were Indonesian territorial waters, the United States challenged this claim but did not precipitate a confrontation with Indonesia, as it might have done in an earlier time, because of larger political considerations. The Suez Canal seizure by Nasser in 1956 produced a significant change in the United States attitude on freedom of international waterways, because it was not prepared to have the issue decided by use of force. This refusal of the United States to condone force clearly indicated that it considered freedom of the seas to be a major, not a vital, interest.[23]

Finally, the United States has supported efforts of the United Nations to station peace-keeping forces in various troubled areas, such as Palestine, the Congo, and Cyprus. However, the United States does not regard United Nations peace-keeping efforts as a vital interest because it has not been willing to use force in support of the United Nations when the Soviet Union was opposed. The United States did not oppose Nasser in 1967 when he demanded that the United Nations force at Sharm el Sheik be with-

---

[23] Even when a similar crisis arose in Panama in 1964, the U.S. was careful not to threaten the use of force against Panama if it took steps to nationalize the canal. In March 1973, when the Panama Canal issue was debated in the United Nations Security Council, the United States carefully avoided any suggestion that it would employ armed forces in the dispute.

drawn, or when he subsequently occupied that strategic area on the Gulf of Aqaba.[24] It might be concluded that the United States considers it a major interest to help the United Nations succeed in ameliorating differences between nations, and even supporting peace-keeping forces financially, but not to the point where it might lead to armed conflict. That is why the United States national interest in the United Nations is at most a major, not a vital, one.[25]

Peripheral interests: Peripheral interests of the United States are those that do not involve a threat to the nation's defense or the well-being of the American people, or seriously affect the stability of the international community. In effect, these are the issues which involve protection of American citizens abroad and the promotion of most private American interests overseas. Examples of peripheral interests are revolutions in certain African and Latin American countries, particularly if Communist organizations are not involved; the expropriation of Americans' private property by foreign governments, if compensation is made; and protection of the rights of United States citizens traveling in foreign countries. Disaster relief usually falls in this category.

In addition to the above, the United States has a peripheral interest in what happens within the territory of the Soviet Union and Communist China, and the countries of Eastern Europe. The cases of Hungary in 1956 and Czechoslovakia in 1968 are examples; in each case, the American people had a deep emotional revulsion to Soviet imposition of control over these two countries, but the United States government did not take any action to prevent the Soviet moves because the risks involved in American intervention in those areas were considered to be greater than the benefits to be gained.[26] We may conclude, then, that the super-

24 The United Nations intervention in Korea was in a somewhat different category because the Soviet Union did not veto the action of the Security Council in June 1950, nor did it threaten to use its own troops in Korea.

25 The United Nations action in the autumn of 1971 to expel the Nationalist Republic of China from membership in favor of the People's Republic further degraded the United Nations in the estimation of many Americans and led to congressional efforts to reduce the U.S. financial contribution to the organization.

26 When the U.S. intervened to crush a revolution in the Dominican Republic in 1965, the Soviet Union did not take any military action to thwart the U.S.

powers implicitly have agreed that the vital interests of the other, insofar as geography is concerned, should be no more than peripheral interests of the other, due to the risk of miscalculation and possible nuclear confrontation. The Middle East is an area where this matter has not yet been resolved.

In addition to the above, the United States has a peripheral interest in building support abroad for its policies and in improving international understanding among peoples. Both objectives derive from the assumption that better understanding among the people of the world, and a clearer appreciation by foreign public opinion of United States objectives, are in its interest. When a United States Information Service library is ransacked by a foreign mob, no retaliation is ever taken because the program is seen as a peripheral interest and therefore not sufficiently important to make an international incident. Thus, it may be said that diplomacy, not coercion or pressure, is used to support peripheral interests. If an issue arose that so deeply involved the property of the United States or of American firms overseas that economic pressure, including cutting off aid, were used, this would indicate immediately that a major, rather than a peripheral, interest was at stake.

If we return then, to the discussion of the four-leveled scale of priorities that can be applied to various international issues, it seems clear that the first and fourth of these degrees of interests – survival and peripheral – are the easiest to define. In the case of a threat to the nation's survival, there is little doubt that the President will do whatever is necessary to protect the country and that a large majority of the American people will unite behind his leadership. Similarly, the United States government usually views strictly private American investments abroad, especially when no national security threat is involved, as a peripheral national interest, requiring diplomatic but not economic pressure. The same is true when there is a change of government in some remote part of the world not considered to be very important to the United States. Tanzania is a good example; the United States

---

there. The strong U.S. response to Soviet moves in Cuba in 1962 probably convinced the Kremlin that its interests in the Western Hemisphere were at best major, not vital.

showed little concern when this African country adopted a pro-Communist policy.

The real problem in defining national interests lies in correctly assessing vital and major interests, i.e., calculating what issues are so important to the basic interests of the nation that the President should be prepared, if all other measures fail to produce the desired result, to use force to protect that interest. If the President decides that an issue is not important enough to risk war, it probably is a major, not a vital, national interest. Another way of viewing it is: if a compromise can be found by which the United States concedes on a point of considerable value to itself, the interest probably is major, not vital. President Johnson's refusal to negotiate with North Vietnam in 1967 was evidence that he perceived a vital interest to be involved in the Vietnam war. Conversely, President Eisenhower's decision in 1954 not to use United States forces in Vietnam was an indication that he did not perceive vital United States interests at that time. President Nixon's policy of disengagement from the Vietnam War indicated that his view of the nation's interests is closer to the Eisenhower view. Similarly, Nixon's handling of economic relations with Japan, Canada, and Europe in 1971–1972 showed that he was prepared to assign a higher priority of interest to advancing American trade and commerce abroad than was his predecessor.

One of the most perplexing problems the United States government has faced in its foreign policy since 1945 is deciding whether its international interests (world order) are compatible with its defense and economic interests.[27] If one views national interests primarily in terms of self-interest, and defines defense, economic well-being and world order narrowly in terms of "what is good for the United States," then it is possible to argue that the United States need not be greatly concerned about the security, economic advancement, and peace of nations in many parts of the world. On the other hand, if one views national interests in broader international terms and accepts a major responsibility for collective security and maintaining world order, then more

[27] See the article by Thomas Cook and Malcolm Moos entitled "The American Idea of International Interest," in Jacobson, *America's Foreign Policy*, p. 135. Reprinted from *American Political Science Review* 47, no. 1 (March 1955): 28–44.

issues in the international environment will be viewed as vital interests of the United States. The United States alliance system, developed in the post–World War II period in response to Soviet expansionism, was a sign of a shift away from a narrow national view to a broad international conception of its national interests.[28]

As the United States enters the mid-1970's, it is clearly redefining its national interests because the old ones, and the assumptions on which they were based, were called into serious question by the experience of the Vietnam War and by the changing nature of the international environment. Nevertheless, the issue is not essentially between isolationism and internationalism in American foreign policy, but the degree of internationalism which the nation is prepared to accept in the coming years. To ask searching questions about what is a vital interest and what is not does not imply a return to isolationism; rather, it suggests a realistic effort to find a path between what many American leaders and scholars believe America's role ought to be and what role the American people are willing to accept over a long period. That is why it is essential for the United States to define more carefully than has been done previously its vital interests in a changing world environment and then marshal the resources of the nation to pursue them successfully. The first Nixon administration made some striking moves toward reorienting United States policy away from Cold-War concepts and toward a more realistic perception of the divisions existing among the great powers. A second Nixon administration is likely to go even further in reordering national interests, most probably in emphasizing economic over defense and world order interests.[29]

[28] The dilemma posed here is articulated admirably in Robert Tucker, *Nation or Empire* (Baltimore, Md., 1968). See also Stanley Hoffmann, *Gulliver's Troubles, or the Setting of American Foreign Policy* (New York, 1968).

[29] The changing perceptions of America's vital national interests in the 1970's are discussed more fully in Ch. 7.

2

Criteria for Determining
Vital Interests

PERHAPS the most pressing need in United States foreign-policy formulation in the 1970's is to define as precisely as possible the criteria to be used in determining what are vital national interests. This is not the same as describing what these vital interests are, or seem to be, or should be; rather, it is the process of asking fundamental questions about what kind of role the United States wishes to play in the world in the final quarter of the twentieth century and what price it is willing to pay to achieve that role.[1] Few scholars and fewer statesmen have attempted a systematic analysis of how this nation arrives at a decision that some values are so important to its well-being that it is willing to go to war, if necessary, to defend or enhance them. The term *vital interest* is used so loosely by political leaders, military officers, journalists, and some scholars that it can mean many things to many people. Some leaders, such as John Foster Dulles, argued that the United States had a vital interest in protecting any nation threatened by Communist aggression and that if military and economic aid were not sufficient to solve the problem, United States armed forces should be used. This was the era of the so-called monolithic Communist menace. Fortunately, that simplistic view of what constitutes a vital national interest is now in disrepute because the United States became aware of the complex nature of the international environment and of the deep divisions among Communist nations. But what measuring stick are we to adopt in the 1970's, what factors ought to be included in the process of deciding that an international issue is, indeed, vital to the national interests of the United States?[2]

There are at least thirteen major factors, or considerations, which should be taken into account by the President and his principal advisers when they are faced with the problem of deciding whether a foreign-policy issue is so important to the interests of the United States that they must contemplate the use of force to solve it if all other measures fail to achieve the desired result. For purposes of discussion, these thirteen factors may be divided into two groups: those primarily concerned with the value the United States attaches to an issue, and those that deal primarily with the costs involved in defending it.

VALUES AND THREATS TO VALUES

1. *Location of the threat:* This is the geographic factor and it applies primarily to the national defense interest – what are the strategic implications for American territory and the people living within United States borders, and for the territory of an ally? If the problem is a Cuba dominated by Castro, or the threat of a Communist-controlled government in the Dominican Republic, the President obviously will consider this to be of greater interest to the United States than a Communist takeover in Laos or in Tanzania, for example. Similarly, insuring that a highly strategic area such as Iceland or Panama is retained in friendly hands is more important to the defense interests of the United States than protection of a country in Central Asia or Central Africa. Geography is no longer so important as it was before ICBM's were perfected because the United States cannot today feel secure only by controlling the oceans off its shores and in maintaining friendly governments in neighboring countries. Nevertheless, the American people and many policy-makers do equate national security with the distance that a trouble spot lies from American territory.

---

[1] Bernard Gordon, in his volume *Toward Disengagement in Asia* (Englewood Cliffs, N.J., 1968), made a useful attempt to look into American history and try to find the answers to why Asia has been a vital interest of the U.S. in this century. Most writers, however, start with the assumption that Europe, Latin America, and the Pacific area are vital U.S. interests and then proceed to discuss what policies are required to defend those interests.

[2] President Nixon's "State of the World" messages to Congress, *U.S. Foreign Policy for the 1970's: Building for Peace* (Washington, D.C., 1971), suggest that he is trying to establish a systematic review of U.S. national interests and objectives for the 1970's and to assess the policies that are needed to achieve them.

That is why the American public found it difficult in 1960–1961 to become alarmed about the possible takeover of Laos or the Congo by local pro-Communist forces, especially after Washington failed to take action to stop the leftward drift of Castro Cuba. Similarly, Nasser's takeover of the Suez Canal in 1956 was viewed with much less alarm in the United States than Panama's threat to nationalize the Panama Canal in 1964. Thus, even though the President may no longer consider geography to be a primary consideration in determining whether a vital United States interest is involved in some issue, he cannot overlook the fact that the public continues to place great weight on this factor and can bring political pressure to bear on him to act or not to act – depending on the distance of the threat from American shores.

2. *Nature of the threat:* It makes a considerable difference in assessing a threat to American security, or to that of an ally, if there is overt, armed aggression across a border, as in Korea in 1950; armed insurgency supported from abroad, as in Greece, Laos, and Vietnam; or an internal struggle for power where both sides appeal for outside support, as in the Congo, Nigeria, or the Dominican Republic. The American people traditionally have opposed the employment of military conquest as a means of changing the status quo abroad, and they can be aroused, as in World War II and in the Korean War, to oppose a blatant aggressor even when the threat is far from American borders. This has been a general principle guiding American policy-makers in formulating policies to deal with open aggression. Indirect aggression, on the other hand, does not entail the same value for the American people, especially if the insurgency is far away. This factor was modified to some extent in the 1950's when Americans were motivated by fear of Communism, wherever it existed in the world. Therefore, the threat of a Communist takeover of a government anywhere in the world, regardless of the means used and the nature of the local Communist movement, was thought to be a threat to the security of the United States; and an effort to save such a threatened state came to be viewed as a vital interest of the United States, regardless of its location. Today, this view of the worldwide Communist threat has undergone considerable revi-

sion, particularly after the Sino-Soviet conflict became apparent in the 1960's. The United States is, therefore, more careful to distinguish between subversion and internal struggles for power, on the one hand, and open aggression across borders when deciding the degree of its own interest.[3]

Political and military threats to United States security are not the only ones that may be considered vital American interests, however. The economic viability of the United States is also crucial: for example, if the nation's currency were seriously threatened by international manipulation, or if other major trading countries adopted policies which endangered the American economy and access to natural resources abroad, this would constitute a vital national interest.[4]

3. *United States economic stake:* When deciding the degree of United States interest toward a foreign area or country, the level of American trade and investment there is an important factor. One of the reasons Japan and Germany probably are vital interests of the United States is because they are among the world's leading industrial powers and are key trading partners of the United States and other major trading nations and could result through Communist conquest or internal political upheaval, would have a profound impact on the economic interests of the United States and other major trading nations and could result in a serious security threat as well. That is why United States policy toward both Germany and Japan changed abruptly after 1950, when it became apparent that the Soviet Union, by its action in Korea, was determined to bring both countries under its influence. Other nations, among them Brazil, Indonesia, Congo, and South Africa, are also important to the United States because of their large natural resources. The vast oil reserves of the Persian Gulf states and the heavy dependence of both Europe and

[3] The Nixon Doctrine, enunciated by the President in the summer of 1969, makes it clear that his administration expects allied countries to bear the major burden of dealing with internal security, which means that he does not consider this kind of problem to be a vital interest of the U.S.

[4] Some critics accused President DeGaulle of trying to manipulate the value of sterling and the dollar and thus weaken Britain's and the U.S.'s political influence in Europe. It is unlikely in the 1970's, however, that the United States would use armed forces to defend strictly economic interests.

Japan on this oil gives this region a special significance on the scale of the United States' national interests; these interests probably will increase in the future because of the growing need of the United States economy for imports of oil.

Economic factors alone usually do not determine whether a country or an area is of vital importance to the United States, yet the economic strength or the economic potential of a country is one of the factors which the President will consider when assessing whether a nation or area is vital to United States interests. If natural resources and markets were the only assets a country had to offer, it would usually rate no higher than a major interest of the United States. South Africa is in this category.

4. *Effect on the balance of power:* A key consideration in any determination of whether a vital interest is at stake is the effect that a failure to act militarily might have on the balance of power in a particular region, or on the strategic balance between the United States and the Soviet Union. President Truman obviously thought that a failure to resist the North Korean attack in 1950 would have jeopardized the security of Japan and emboldened the Soviets to press their political offensive in Europe. Similarly, President Eisenhower concluded in 1958 that a failure to act decisively in the Middle East might have given Nasser, with Soviet support, the courage to launch an attack on Israel and to take control of the oil concessions in the area. President Kennedy came away from his Vienna 1961 confrontation with Chairman Khrushchev convinced that a failure to reinforce Berlin would create a serious situation in that beleaguered city and in the rest of Europe. And President Johnson's decision in 1965 to use American ground forces to prevent the collapse of South Vietnam was strongly influenced by his concern that a failure to act there would destroy the balance of power in Southeast Asia and eventually result in its domination by Hanoi and Peking. In each of these cases, the President perceived United States interests to be vitally affected, not because of the single country whose security was threatened, but because he anticipated a serious threat to the balance of power in the area and a test of America's determination to maintain the balance.

The Cuban Missile Crisis in 1962 and the United States decision in 1968 to deploy an antiballistic missile system are in a somewhat different category, but no less vital to American interests. In these cases, the strategic balance between the Soviet Union and the United States was being threatened, and Presidents Kennedy and Johnson concluded that they could not afford to permit the Soviet Union to gain such an advantage over the United States because they feared that the Soviets would use it to intimidate the United States. President Nixon came to the same conclusion in 1969 when he decided to proceed with deployment of the multiple independently targeted reentry vehicle (MIRV) to American strategic forces. In a word, if the Soviets could gain superiority in the strategic balance of power, they would use it to force the United States to concede on other matters of vital interest. This factor, the worldwide balance of strategic power, is one which presidents and their diplomatic and military advisers are deeply concerned about even though the public often is not aware of, or does not appreciate, that this factor must be a vital interest. Protection of the strategic balance of power is a value which must be weighed in determining what is vital, and there is no precise way of assessing what degree of value should be attached in any given circumstance.

5. *Effect on worldwide United States credibility and prestige:* The term *prestige,* like the term *national interest,* is widely used by statesmen, strategists, and scholars, but its precise meaning in international politics is elusive and, therefore, it is open to misunderstanding among the general public. Prestige results from being respected by other nations, and respect is gained in the international community by wisely employing the tools of power and diplomacy to pursue legitimate national interests. For a great power such as the United States, prestige is gained by providing wise leadership to an alliance system and protecting lesser powers in the alliance against external dangers. When Secretary of State Rusk talked of the "credibility" of the United States' word in international affairs, he meant that defending allied nations dependent on American power for their survival was a matter of great importance to United States prestige and perhaps honor.

The willingness of the United States to use nuclear weapons in the event another nuclear power launched an attack on an ally is an essential ingredient in its postwar deterrence policy vis-à-vis the Soviet Union. Therefore, the credibility of this nuclear deterrent, the willingness to use it in retaliation, is an important element in maintaining United States worldwide prestige.

As in considerations of balance of power, the President is heavily influenced in deciding the existence of a vital interest by what is likely to be the reaction of both friends and foes if he decides not to take bold actions, but relies instead on diplomacy to solve the problem. Will his course be perceived as a sign of weakness by both ally and potential enemies? Will his failure to act in one situation mean that he is going to be tested even more in another and perhaps less attractive place? President Kennedy probably found himself in such a situation in Laos early in 1961 when he decided to negotiate that problem with the Soviet Union rather than use military force. Most Asian capitals read his decision as a sign of weakness, and within a short time Vietnam replaced Laos as the test of United States prestige in Asia. Conversely, President Nixon's bold, albeit risky, incursion into Cambodia in 1970 caused Asian nations to take his policies in Vietnam seriously.

6. *Historical sentiment of the American people:* Every nation has certain cultural and psychological attachments for other peoples and countries that affect the policies of their governments, and the United States probably has a greater variety of attachments because of the unique character of its population. Every minority group in the United States, with the possible exception of the Negroes, has maintained sentimental ties with the mother country for at least one generation, and some have continued strong cultural ties over a longer period of time. These attachments have had a significant influence on United States policy because they constitute a political constraint in assessing the national interest. The strong Anglo-Saxon tradition of the United States was an important factor in the decisions of Presidents Wilson and Roosevelt to enter two world wars on the side of Great Britain. Roosevelt's decision in World War II to defend Aus-

tralia was based, in part, on cultural and political attachments to the Australian people.[5]

The large Jewish minority in the United States and its strong attachments to the state of Israel is probably the most dramatic example of ethnic and cultural ties influencing the assessment of the degree of United States national interests. President Truman was heavily influenced by this when he decided to recognize a Jewish state of Israel in 1948, despite the misgivings of many of his advisers.[6] The difference in views between American oil companies and the American Jewish community over what the national interest in the Middle East ought to be has caused all postwar presidents considerable difficulty in trying to formulate foreign policy concerning that region. Again, the sentiment of important groups of Americans is a value that must be weighed by the President and his advisers in assessing national interests, and it is often decided on domestic political grounds, rather than on the basis of other considerations.

7. *Attitude of major allies and the United Nations:* All postwar American presidents have taken account of the views of key allies and have sought to minimize potential opposition in the United Nations when deciding to use armed forces abroad. This was particularly true with Presidents Truman and Eisenhower, both of whom placed considerable value on avoiding unilateral military intervention abroad and seeking collective action with allies when vital interests were at stake. Presidents Kennedy and Johnson put less value on the concept of collective defense, one reason being that in the 1960's the relative power of the United States was far superior to that of its major allies – Britain and France – and their military support was considered of marginal importance when deciding on American military intervention. This was pointed up after the ill-fated Suez intervention in 1956, when France and, to a lesser extent, Britain began to draw away from

---

[5] The strong influence of Irish and German minorities, however, probably caused Wilson to wait longer than he might otherwise have done to enter the war on the side of the Allies in World War I.

[6] See Dean Acheson, *Present at the Creation* (New York, 1969).

support of United States policy and concentrated their efforts on problems closer to Europe.[7]

President Truman took particular care to get United Nations support for his decision to intervene in the Korean War, and President Eisenhower gave as one reason for not intervening in Vietnam in 1954 the unwillingness of the British government to save the French colonial empire in Southeast Asia. Eisenhower sought United Nations endorsement for his policy in Lebanon in 1958 and in the Congo in 1960. President Kennedy also sought United Nations support for his policies, but unlike his predecessors he downgraded the value of both British and French support in Asia. President Johnson minimized the importance of both the United Nations and his European allies, and sought instead to gain Asian support for his policies in Vietnam. President Nixon continued the policy of limited support for the activities of the United Nations, but he placed greater value on gaining the support of European allies for his policies in Asia as well as in Europe.

From a strictly military standpoint, no American President in the post–World War II period needed the support of either European or Asian allies, but during the late 1940's and 1950's the United States required overseas bases for its strategic air power in order to carry out its policy of containment. The territory of nations around the periphery of the so-called Communist bloc was important for the deployment of United States military power, and allies were therefore sought and supported with generous amounts of military and economic assistance. In the 1960's, however, these bases were no longer essential for basing strategic forces, and the need for providing large military and economic aid programs to these countries declined. Thailand and the Philippines were exceptions, however, as their territory was essential to the prosecution of the Vietnam War.

Even though the military importance of allies may have declined, their political importance has not diminished. This is be-

---

[7] The Laotian crisis of 1960–1961 clearly showed that neither the British nor the French was prepared to use armed forces to back up their SEATO treaty obligations in Laos.

cause American presidents have found it politically desirable to explain policies of intervention – especially those far from American territory – to the American people in terms of collective action by free world countries, rather than in terms of United States interests alone. The reason is that many Americans continue to view the world in idealistic terms and are prepared to support military actions abroad only if the President can demonstrate altruistic motives, not selfish national interests.[8] Liberal thought in the United States usually opposes unilateral military action by the United States, which is interpreted to be imperialism or power politics. On the other hand, armed action in the cause of peace, especially when other nations share in the responsibility, greatly reduces the influence of those who oppose all military action except in case of national survival. In World Wars I and II, Presidents Wilson and Roosevelt went to great lengths to show the American people that the wars were being fought for universal objectives, not for narrow selfish interests. President Truman made a similar effort during the Korean War to convince the public that it was a "just war." However, Presidents Kennedy, Johnson, and Nixon could not convince the American public that Vietnam was in that category. Public disillusionment over the Vietnam War raises the question whether the public will support any limited war in the foreseeable future that is not in response to a direct threat to United States territory.

Thus, one may conclude that the importance of having allies and gaining United Nations support is a political rather than a military consideration for a President. If he can show the American people that they are fighting in a just cause that is shared, or at least supported, by other major nations, he is more likely to obtain public support than if his actions are perceived to be unilateral. This factor applies only to actions that are not in the survival category, because in that case the views of allies would not be very important to a President. The Cuban Missile Crisis was one of those cases.

[8] See Robert E. Osgood, *Ideals and Self-Interest in America's Foreign Relations* (Chicago, 1953), for a detailed description of the historical basis of this phenomenon.

Costs and Risks of Deeper Involvement

Thus far, we have discussed factors that fall under the heading of values a prudent President should take into consideration when assessing the degree of national interest involved in an international issue. Once values are attached to these seven factors, the President and his advisers ought then to be concerned with cost factors – with the problem of assessing whether the costs and risks of intervention outweigh the benefit to be derived. The following six factors fall into this cost category.

1. *Anticipated economic costs of intervention:* Few presidents are willing to send United States forces overseas into combat without having a reasonably clear idea of what the operation is likely to cost. American military forces, unlike those of many other countries, are highly mobile, but they are also very expensive to move and to supply. Part of this has to do with the kind of equipment and supplies accompanying American forces when they are deployed overseas. Another part of the cost involves the relatively large pay and allowances the troops receive when they are in combat zones, and United States military tactics of using expensive machines rather than manpower wherever possible to dislodge an enemy from a position also contributes to the high cost of military operations. This reduces casualties but increases financial costs, as the destruction of planes and helicopters by enemy forces in the Vietnam War shows. Determining the financial costs of a military deployment also involves a calculation of the duration of the conflict, and this part of the equation is not always predictable. Therefore, the President must rely heavily on his military and intelligence advisers to help him estimate costs. If he concludes, as President Truman did in 1950–1951, that the war may not end quickly, he must then decide whether to impose wage and price controls on the economy, in order to reduce inflationary pressure, and to ask Congress for increased taxes to pay for the war. Such actions are usually unpopular in Congress. If the President concludes, as Lyndon Johnson apparently did in 1965–1966, that it will not be a long war, he may prosecute the conflict without resort to economic controls or increased taxes

in the expectation that the increased military costs can be absorbed for a short time. He may also calculate that Congress will not refuse him the funds while American soldiers are in combat.

Balance-of-payments considerations must also be taken into account, because foreign wars involve the purchase of supplies and services outside the United States and thus increase the outflow of dollars to foreign countries. In the Korean and Vietnam wars, foreign civilian labor was employed to support United States forces; also, American troops spend a considerable share of their pay in foreign countries, on Rest and Recreation leave and on foreign products. Balance of payments is not an important consideration when the duration of an intervention is expected to be short, as was the case in Lebanon in 1958 and in the Dominican Republic in 1965; however, when American forces are sent into combat and the end of fighting is uncertain – as in Korea and Vietnam – the economic costs of maintaining a large force overseas should be carefully considered before intervention is decided upon.

2. *Anticipated human costs:* This is perhaps the most crucial of the cost factors the President must take into account when deciding whether a foreign threat is of such importance that he must be prepared to use armed force to influence the outcome. Not only must he calculate the number of military casualties that might be sustained, but he must also take into account the strains that will be placed on the domestic economy as a result of the increased manpower requirements for the armed forces and defense industries. This is especially important if he is obliged to call up reserve units, as occurred during the Korean War and in 1968 during the Vietnam conflict when air reserve units were sent to Korea following the capture of the U.S.S. *Pueblo.*

Large casualties on a foreign battlefield, particularly when there is no declaration of war, are difficult for the American people to accept unless the security of the United States is clearly threatened. Americans tend to be impatient about ending wars and limited interventions so that the President can "bring the boys home." The large number of casualties plus the inconclusiveness of the interventions probably contributed more than any other factor to the disenchantment among the American people over the Korean and the Vietnam conflicts. At the beginning of these interventions, there was general consensus in the country that use of American forces to prevent the military collapse of the South Korean and South Vietnamese governments was in the national interest. However, when the Chinese intervened in the Korean conflict and American casualties mounted, opposition began to be heard at home and President Truman came under increasing criticism for his handling of the war; Dwight Eisenhower used this as a principal issue in the presidential campaign in 1952. The growing number of United States casualties in Vietnam, even though they were far fewer than those of Vietcong and North Vietnamese forces, produced increasing opposition to the war in 1966 and 1967, particularly from among young draft-age men. On the other hand, the interventions in Lebanon in 1958 and in the Dominican Republic in 1965 did not result in more than a few casualties, and as these troops were withdrawn within a few months, there was no serious opposition to either intervention from the American public.[9]

The North Vietnamese Communist leadership seemed to be well aware of the relationship between battlefield casualties and American patience in fighting limited wars. Some of their tactics in Vietnam were clearly designed to increase United States casualties and to dramatize them in the United States. Their own enormous casualties apparently had little impact on Hanoi's determination to force an American withdrawal from Vietnam. Although General William Westmoreland professed to be fighting a war of attrition against the Communist forces, it seems that the North Vietnamese leadership had a similar strategy in mind: they apparently concluded that if they did not sue for peace but instead inflicted several thousand casualties on United States forces every week, the American public would tire of the conflict and demand that the President bring an end to the fighting. Secretary

---

[9] It should be noted, however, that there was serious press criticism of the Johnson administration for using U.S. forces in the Dominican Republic because, it was argued, no foreign threat was involved there. This opposition, however, did not affect the general public, as did the Korean and Vietnamese conflicts, because the material and human costs of the Dominican intervention were small.

of State Rusk had this factor in mind when he characterized criticism of the war within the United States as playing into the enemy's hands.

Because of the relationship of American casualties to battlefield tactics, no nation has used machines to better advantage in warfare than did the United States in Vietnam. Still, when battle deaths reached four hundred and five hundred a week in 1967 and affected many communities across the United States, the public reaction was reflected in mounting congressional criticism of the war. During World War II, many more casualties were incurred in fighting the German and Japanese forces, but the American people were willing to make those sacrifices because they perceived the survival of the nation to be at stake. In Vietnam and in Korea no such perception of danger prevailed, and the human costs were probably the first measure of whether either war could be fought for limited objectives without bringing the government into serious difficulty with the public.

3. *Effectiveness of military action in solving a problem:* Even if the President and a majority of the Congress conclude that a foreign crisis presents so serious a threat to United States national interests that force must be contemplated to protect that interest, this still leaves open the question of whether military intervention is the only, or even a feasible, means of achieving the objective. Many serious foreign-policy issues have been faced by this country in the postwar period, and many were solved without the use of ground forces. In some cases these situations were dealt with through skillful diplomacy, as in Indonesia during the rule of Sukarno.[10] In other cases, such as the far-leftist Arbenz government in Guatemala and the Mossadegh regime in Iran, clandestine operations rather than military intervention proved successful in bringing about a change in government. Such efforts are not always successful, however, as was shown by the Bay of Pigs fiasco in Cuba.

10 U.S. policy there was to give Sukarno enough rope to hang himself, on the assumption that the Indonesian army would fight rather than let the Communist PKI take over control of the country. Skillful diplomacy and continued assistance to the Indonesian army from 1962 to 1965 proved successful when the "crunch" with the PKI came in 1965.

It seems clear that military force, or the threatened use of military force, is a realistic policy only to the extent that the problem is essentially a military one and can be dealt with by conventional military forces. If the problem basically is of a political nature, or is one requiring primarily police action, military forces might then be of only marginal utility and, indeed, might even be counterproductive. For example, there was little doubt that the threat to Berlin in the postwar period was a military one and that the introduction of additional ground forces there in 1961 was an effective means of warning the Soviet Union and East Germany that they would have to fight to take over that city. The same was true insofar as the defense of Western Europe was concerned in 1951 when President Truman sent General Eisenhower there to organize the joint NATO command. The problem was similar in Korea when President Truman sent American forces into combat. But this was clearly not the case in Vietnam in the early 1960's because the nature of the conflict there was essentially political – just as it was in Malaya when the British had to deal with an insurgency there in the 1950's, and in the Philippines when the government had to cope with the Hukbalahap (HUK) problem. It can probably be argued that the conflict in China in the late 1940's was also in this category and that the United States government wisely decided that the introduction of military forces there would not affect the outcome of that revolutionary struggle, unless it was willing to use atomic weapons.

President Kennedy seemed to recognize this factor when he decided to institute counterinsurgency training programs in the army to train military units (Green Berets) in the unconventional warfare tactics adopted by Communist forces in Southeast Asia, and which Castro was trying to export to Latin American countries. In the early 1970's President Nixon seemed to be relying more on balance-of-power diplomacy and on nuclear deterrence to protect American interests abroad.

Any great power, especially a superpower, must insure that when it employs military forces in support of a vital interest the action will quickly achieve the desired result. If it miscalculates and the military operation is not pursued to a successful conclusion, this can be politically if not militarily disastrous to its reputation as a great power and may result in instability in the international system. This is what happened to the British and French governments when they sought unsuccessfully to crush Nasser in 1956; they did not mount sufficient force to achieve their objective quickly, and as a result their prestige and roles in the world suffered a severe blow when the superpowers stepped in and forced their withdrawal from Egyptian territory. A similar humiliation, although not of the same magnitude, took place when President Kennedy decided not to intervene in Laos in 1961, after publicly warning the Soviet Union that he might do so if it did not persuade the Pathet Lao forces there to stop their military offensive toward the Mekong River. He suffered another humiliation in Cuba that spring by not standing behind the Cuban insurgents who were trained in the United States and transported to the Bay of Pigs in American ships. This is not to argue that Kennedy should have used United States forces to invade Cuba, but to point out the danger a great power runs when it starts a military operation that it either is not able to finish or is unwilling to support beyond a certain point. In contrast with these cases, the Soviet intervention in Czechoslovakia in 1968 and the United States intervention in the Dominican Republic in 1965 were operations that achieved their objectives in a short time with minimum bloodshed and little equivocation by either superpower. President Nixon's decision in 1972 to mine Haiphong Harbor was another example. Although each action was deplored by the other power, and by a large segment of the world community, both powers demonstrated their willingness to use military power effectively to defend important interests.

4. *Probable duration of conflict:* Another factor the President must assess when deciding whether and what kinds of military forces he should use to defend a vital interest is the tenacity of the enemy. If he calculates that the enemy is weak, a military show of force may bring the desired result. In some cases, sending the Sixth or Seventh Fleet into troubled areas has been sufficient indication of United States intentions to achieve the desired result. A strong diplomatic note may also be sufficient evidence of Amer-

ican concern to convince a potential enemy to pull back from a dangerous position. However, in dealing with revolutionary situations, where the motivation of peoples is an important factor, the President and his chief advisers must take into account the likelihood that the enemy may not respond positively to the use, or threatened use, of military force. In revolutionary warfare, a people and their government may be willing to suffer large casualties and endure great hardship rather than submit to foreign military power. The Vietnam and Malayan insurgencies are prime examples. This was true also in Germany and Japan during World War II, for saturation bombing of both countries did not alone bring an end to those wars; in Germany it took the combined armed forces of Britain, the Soviet Union, and the United States to insure Hitler's final defeat, and in Japan the war ended only when the United States used a superweapon and threatened to demolish all Japanese cities.

For a power such as the United States, the question must be raised whether the limited use of military force in distant parts of the world will be effective in bringing a revolutionary enemy to terms before the American people tire of the war and demand the withdrawal of United States forces. Although many other factors were involved in the Vietnam equation, it can be argued that the determination of the North Vietnamese to pursue the struggle regardless of costs was predictable in 1965, given the history of their struggle against the French and the kind of infrastructure they had built up in South Vietnam. It might also be argued that Chinese intervention in the Korean War was predictable in 1950 and that Peking was prepared to suffer great casualties to prevent the United States from threatening its border at the Yalu River. This is not to say that the United States should have refused to intervene in either situation; however, a better appreciation of the intentions of the enemy and his determination to fight against considerable odds might have caused the President to adopt different strategies in dealing with these situations. For example, if it had been known in advance that bombing North Vietnamese military targets would have little effect on ending the war in the South, would the President have risked the protests both at home and abroad when United States planes hit civilian targets by mistake?

In sum, when the President contemplates the use of armed force to protect or advance a national interest, he should correctly assess whether limited military intervention will accomplish the desired result in a reasonably short period. Assuming that an all-out military effort is not contemplated, i.e., if a survival interest is not at stake, he should correctly calculate whether the limited use of force will cause an enemy to negotiate. If he has reason to think that (1) the enemy will not be persuaded by a limited application of force, (2) the American public will not support a protracted limited war with substantial casualties, and (3) the interest involved is not worth the risk of confrontation with another superpower, the President may conclude that the issue involved is of only major, not a vital, interest to the United States and should not, therefore, involve the use of ground forces. This does not preclude the presence of navy and air force units in the general area of conflict, however, to "show the flag."

5. *Risks of enlarged war:* Any President who contemplates using military forces abroad to protect a vital interest must take into account the risks he runs of enlarging the war and bringing the United States into direct confrontation with the only other power which in the mid-1970's could inflict destruction on the United States – the Soviet Union. If the objective is to keep the intervention limited in scope, the President will seek to reassure other major powers that their vital interests are not endangered and that a military response is neither warranted nor desirable. At the same time, however, the President should not proceed on the assumption that other powers will refrain from intervention; he must, therefore, be prepared for a larger war if one occurs. Although this factor may not be given much publicity, its assessment probably occupies more man-hours of various executive agencies engaged in foreign-policy decision-making than any other single factor analyzed here, for the nature of the current "balance of terror" between the superpowers requires that any President weigh carefully the extent to which the use of armed

force will threaten the vital interests of the Soviet Union, or China, and result in their taking military actions in response. There is probably no instance in the post–World War II period when the United States felt it could act with impunity against the Soviet Union, even before the U.S.S.R. broke the atomic monopoly of the United States in 1949. When the Soviets blockaded the rail and highway communications with West Berlin in 1948, the United States chose to employ an airlift rather than run the risk of starting a war by sending an armored column through the Soviet occupation zone of Germany, as some presidential advisers proposed.

To list some of the foreign-policy crises in which the United States has been involved in the past quarter century is to dramatize the importance of correctly calculating Soviet intentions: Truman's intervention in Korea in 1950, Eisenhower's decision not to intervene in Indochina in 1954, the Taiwan Strait Crisis of 1958, the Congo in 1960–1961, the Cuban Missile Crisis in 1962, the Second Vietnam War, and the Arab-Israel War of 1967.[11] One of the reasons why the United States dealt so cautiously with the conflict in the Middle East in 1967 was that it wished to avoid a confrontation with the Soviet Union, whose interests in that area are much greater than in Southeast Asia, and because the United States may not have been prepared to send its own forces to the area unless there was clear evidence that the Soviets intended to use military power to gain control of the Eastern Mediterranean area. Nixon's calculated risk in 1972 in mining Haiphong Harbor in North Vietnam was based on his correct perception that the Soviet Union had a greater interest in pursuing a detente with the United States than in enlarging the Vietnam War.

Today, the Soviet Union is the only real threat to the security of the continental United States and it occupies the greatest attention of policy-makers when the question of deploying United

---

[11] In this latter crisis, it was reported that President Johnson used the hot line to Moscow to assure Soviet leaders that the U.S. did not intend to intervene in that conflict. The Cuban Missile Crisis is probably the best example of the agonizing considerations that go into a presidential decision to risk confrontation with the USSR.

States forces abroad is contemplated. However, Communist China's intentions have also loomed large in United States calculations since 1950, when President Truman misjudged the Chinese response to his decision to permit General Douglas MacArthur to move into North Korea late that year. The lesson was not lost on Presidents Kennedy and Johnson when they made decisions about increasing the size of the American military commitment to South Vietnam in the 1960's. One of the main reasons President Johnson did not use United States forces to invade North Vietnam was his fear that such action might bring in large Chinese forces and, perhaps, cause the Soviet Union to use military pressure against United States interests in Europe and the Middle East. When the United States reacted adversely to British and French intervention in Egypt in 1956, one of the reasons was concern that the Soviet Union might use this as a pretext to move against Berlin, Greece, or Turkey.[12] When President Eisenhower sent United States forces to Lebanon in 1958, he sought to reassure the Soviet Union that this action did not threaten its vital interests.

Although the President must assess the risks of Soviet or Chinese military retaliation whenever he decides to intervene in a foreign area, he must also take into account what could be the longer-term risks to the security of the United States if it does not respond when its commitments or prestige is challenged. This consideration is particularly important to a great power that has assumed a worldwide peace-keeping role, as the United States has done during the post–World War II period, for the credibility of that role rests on the willingness of the peace-keeper to act wherever and whenever peace is endangered. In this context, the consideration of risks of an enlarged conflict resulting from military intervention is intertwined with concern for maintaining a regional balance of power. The President may be less concerned with the immediate threat to a given country far removed from the United States than with the conclusions Soviet and Chinese leaders might draw from his failure to aid a country which is con-

---

[12] It apparently did embolden the Kremlin to crush the Hungarian revolt, however.

sidered to be within the United States' sphere of influence. It was for this reason that President Kennedy was preoccupied, somewhat ludicrously, with tiny Laos during the first three months of his administration, to the point where he publicly warned the Soviet Union not to push that situation too far.

The importance of this factor, risks of an enlarged war, is likely to grow in importance if nuclear proliferation intensifies. This may mean that the President will not be willing to intervene in certain areas if a nuclear confrontation could result. This situation will clearly call for a closer assessment in the future of the possible costs of deciding that an issue is vital to the United States. If the likely or potential costs of armed intervention to support non-Communist governments is thought to be too high, the probability is that a greater number of situations formerly perceived as vital to United States security will be considered major in the future.

6. *Reaction of public opinion and Congress:* In the final analysis, no President can pursue foreign policies or define national interests that are at variance with the basic values of the American people, unless he has little regard for either his own or his political party's future. This is not to say that the President cannot at times take foreign-policy decisions which run counter to public sentiment and to the views of Congress: the Constitution clearly gives him considerable authority as Commander-in-Chief and as the dominant voice in foreign-policy matters to use independent judgment when crises arise or when the country is divided.[13] But a prudent President knows that if his policies are out of touch with the prevailing or predictable sentiments of the American people, he and his party run the large risk of being repudiated at the polls.[14] Presidents cannot for long ignore public opinion also because they will need congressional support to

[13] President Roosevelt clearly took measures in 1941 to aid the British which went beyond what either Congress or the public felt was justified because he perceived that the vital interests of the nation were at stake.

[14] President Nixon said in explaining his decision to send U.S. forces into Cambodia in May 1970 that he would rather be a one-term president than let his judgment of what is best for the country be decided by public opinion at the moment.

obtain funds needed for carrying out a foreign intervention.[15]

Public and congressional support for the President's foreign policies is heavily influenced by other factors, particularly the duration of the conflict, the number of casualties, and the historical sentiments of the American people. The average citizen is not greatly concerned about the conduct of American foreign policy as long as there are no serious problems. Generally, he is willing to leave it to the President to determine what is best for the country, and during the 1940's and 1950's, when the United States concluded defense alliances with many countries around the world, there was little opposition from the public or in Congress. Yet, when these treaties were put to the test in Southeast Asia, the public became aroused because the cost of carrying them out became excessive.[16] The public is particularly sensitive to American foreign interventions when young draftees are sent to a distant country where no historical ties or sentiments of the American people are involved. So long as the risk of prolonged fighting remains small, the President probably can absorb the attacks of congressional critics because the public may not become aroused if the intervention is brought quickly to a successful conclusion. If the President cannot convince the public that an early end to the war is in sight, he runs the risk of being caught in a growing polarization of public opinion: those who clamor for a greater war effort to force an enemy to capitulate, and those who press for disengagement from the struggle through a negotiated settlement, which means giving the enemy more concessions than some segments of the public believe to be honorable. Both the Korean and the Vietnam wars proved to be exceedingly difficult political dilemmas for Presidents Truman, Johnson, and Nixon to resolve because of the inconclusive nature of the struggles.

The nature of the American political system is seen by some

[15] In the summer of 1970, it was apparent that Congress delayed several key legislative proposals of the President, as well as some appointments, because of its dissatisfaction with his decision to send forces into Cambodia.

[16] In Korea, the U.S. had no treaty commitment to defend Korea, but President Truman decided that a vital interest was at stake because of the implications of a Communist victory there for the future political orientation of Japan and for the security of Europe.

as the Achilles heel of American efforts to be leader of the non-Communist world. The question must seriously be asked in the 1970's whether the American people will permit any future President to determine the national interest and to commit American troops to foreign battle without the kind of national debate which was envisioned by the founding fathers. The "revolt" of the Senate in May and June of 1970, which resulted in its passage of the Cooper-Church Amendment to the Foreign Military Assistance Act, was evidence of growing public anxiety over permitting any President to exercise sole judgment on when and where to send armed forces into battle. It might be argued that the high-water mark of American preeminence as a world power was reached in early 1968 and that it has been receding since that time because the United States political system refused to permit the President to exercise freedom of action in carrying out a role of international policeman. Even though an individual President may choose to ignore public sentiment on what he considers to be the vital national interests of the country, in the final analysis, the American people will pass judgment when they elect a President.[17] The reelection of Richard Nixon in 1972 was evidence that the American people believed he would not involve the country in another Vietnam-type conflict and also that he would seek to reduce world tensions by active diplomacy with both Moscow and Peking.

In this discussion of the criteria that should be examined before a determination is made that an issue is a vital United States interest, we have concentrated on one of the three basic national interests described in Chapter 1, namely, national defense. This is perhaps natural in view of American preoccupation with national security issues in the quarter-century following World War II. There were many reasons for this overriding concern for national defense, often at the expense of other interests, but one factor seems to stand out above the others: the generation of Americans that fought and won the great wars against Germany and Japan was determined in 1945 that this nation should never

[17] See Ch. 3 for a more detailed discussion of presidential authority in determining national interests.

again be placed in the position of military weakness that had characterized its situation in the 1930's and led, many were convinced, to the conclusion by the Axis Powers that the United States would not fight to prevent their domination of Europe and the Pacific. After the war, when the Soviet Union began to show aggressive tendencies in Europe, there was little public opposition to President Truman's call for rearmament and for increased production of atomic and nuclear weapons. Postwar leaders were persuaded that the Soviet Union constituted a grave military threat to the United States and had to be contained with military power, and the Eisenhower administration continued the build-up of American strategic power. The armed forces were strengthened even further in the Kennedy and Johnson administrations.

The American people accepted this large investment in military power because the age group that participated in World War II held the reins of economic and political power in the postwar period. The nation's foreign-policy leaders in this period – Dean Acheson, John Foster Dulles, Averell Harriman, Dean Rusk, to name a few – were adherents of the "realist" school of international politics; they were convinced that the willingness to use massive military power was the only way the United States could deal with Soviet and Chinese pressure and maintain America's leadership role in the world.

However, a new generation of Americans came to maturity in the 1960's and did not necessarily share this view of the world or accept the heavy reliance on military power as the means of maintaining international peace. These young people were much more concerned about the danger of nuclear annihilation, because the superpowers had failed to reach a comprehensive understanding about limitation of nuclear armaments. They were less concerned about economic security and felt freer to criticize what they considered to be the materialism of American society and reliance on instruments of mass destruction to maintain world order. They protested against defining national interests primarily in defense and security terms and insisted that much greater attention be given to promoting world peace and freedom and providing for resolution of conflict without resort to violence.[18] The more moderate critics of United States foreign policy argued that defense ought not to be the overriding national interest, that establishing an accommodation with other powers is far more important to long-term United States interests. In effect, the protest movement of the 1960's (which greatly diminished in the early 1970's) set the stage for a thorough reappraisal of United States national interests by the Nixon administration.

If we use the factors outlined earlier in this chapter to test the degree of interest the United States has in maintaining a peaceful world order, we can get another view of what constitutes a vital national interest. For example, one can make a case, using these considerations, that it was a vital interest for the United States to insure that United Nations peace-keeping forces took over the security role in the Congo in the early 1960's. Also, most of the thirteen factors described above for deciding whether United States military forces should ultimately be employed might be used to determine which policy to follow in order to reduce the risks of nuclear confrontation with the Soviet Union and nuclear proliferation among other countries. In this case, maintenance of world order would be the overriding consideration, rather than containment of Communist power and influence; there likely would be much greater emphasis on skillful diplomacy, foreign aid, and technical assistance than on military power and clandestine operations as instruments of national policy. This could mean a decline in the importance of allies and suggest that greater efforts should be made to "build bridges" to hostile and neutral countries. It would also promote a multipolar world rather than the bipolar one that dominated international relations for nearly twenty-five years; but it might also result in a shift of United States policy from preoccupation with international affairs to domestic priorities. This would not necessarily mean a return to isolationism as it was known in the 1920's and 1930's, but it would surely result in a shifting of priorities away from concentration on America's world role. The attractive-

---

[18] They also insisted that the government give greater attention to the domestic needs of the nation and curtail what they believed to be an imbalance in national priorities in favor of defense and space exploration.

ness of this view of national interests appears to be growing, especially among the post–World War II generation.

A third fundamental national interest, promotion of United States trade and investment overseas, is another which has not received the attention it deserves in the postwar period. There were two main reasons: one, in the early postwar period, the United States had a surplus of both agricultural and industrial products, and the rest of the world was prostrate from the war. The United States also had most of the world's gold supply and the problem was to find suitable ways of distributing this wealth in order to stimulate international trade and commerce and re-establish a strong international monetary system. Another factor was America's preoccupation with defense and security, which made considerations of balance of payments, foreign competition, and gold flows seem less important than the military and economic well-being of United States allies.[19]

The maintenance of a strong world economic position for the United States is considered by a growing number of Americans to be a vital national interest. They have history on their side, because until World War II the promotion of American trade and commerce was considered by many United States leaders to be more important than national defense and world order. The idea that American forces should be used for international peace-keeping was anathema to most American leaders prior to World War II. In the 1970's, the economic interest is getting increasing attention as foreign competition with United States exports increases, and as foreign imports into United States markets expand at an alarming rate in certain areas, such as textiles, shoes, and electronics, and cause serious concern among domestic producers and American labor.[20]

---

[19] The effect on the U.S. balance of payments of maintaining military bases and large forces overseas in the 1960's was a reminder of the economic price that must be paid for the assumption of a policeman's role in international relations.

[20] The growing problem of imports from Japan received considerable public attention in the early 1970's and resulted in increased pressures on Congress to enact quota restrictions on certain foreign goods. Also, the Assistant Secretary of Commerce for International Affairs resigned his post because of what he considered to be a lack of attention to this growing problem by the Nixon administration. But by summer 1971, the President reversed his policy and began to exert pressure on Japan to revalue the yen and lift its restrictive trade practices against the U.S.

Although the list of criteria used to define vital interests in national defense might not fit precisely a definition of what is a vital economic interest, some of the same considerations can be applied. For example, the size and location of a foreign market, its effect on the total trade of the United States, the attachment of American people to goods from certain sources, the intensity of competition and the effect on the world balance of trade, the availability of goods from other sources, the attitude of other countries – all these factors could be applied to the United States interest in trade, commerce, and investment, as well as in national security. The case of Japan is a good example of where vital economic interests may come into conflict with vital world-order interests: it is clearly a vital national interest of the United States to keep Japan as a politically stable ally, because of United States interests in East Asia and the Pacific, but this consideration is tempered by the fact that the American trade imbalance with Japan has been growing and domestic producers are pressuring Congress and the President to give them relief from Japanese competition. The fact that the United States provides for most of Japan's defense only exacerbates the problem. Thus, it will be a major task for the United States government in the future to bring the nation's economic and security interests more into harmony, and this may well result in a reduction in its treaty commitments and military facilities in many parts of the world.

In summary, the need to define more precisely what is meant by vital interests is an urgent one, no matter whether the interest is defense, economic, or world order. If the United States is in process of reorienting the focus of its basic interests to accommodate the realities and perspectives of the 1970's, it is no less important that the new interests be defined in terms which the American people will accept and support. Without a broad consensus of public support, no interest – even if completely logical to policy makers – will be defensible in the American political system. That is why more precise definitions of national interests are required and more analytical tools are needed to determine the relationship between interests and policies.

3

Roles of the President and Congress in Determining Interests

THE QUESTION of who should have the primary responsibility for determining United States national interests has been debated from the beginnings of the Republic. The founding fathers grappled with this problem in much the same manner they debated other questions related to the powers to be accorded the President, which should go to Congress and the courts, and which should be retained by the states. As on many other issues, Hamilton and Madison were the spokesmen for two opposite views: Hamilton argued that in foreign affairs the President must be given great latitude in determining vital national interests because it was essential that the nation be able to speak with one voice in an international environment dominated by great-power politics. Madison contended that Congress should have the major voice in determining the nation's interests because it had the power to declare war and raise armies. Edwin Corwin came to the conclusion in his study of the presidency that "the verdict of history, in short, is that the power to determine the substantive content of American foreign policy is a divided power, with the lion's share falling usually, though by no means always, to the President."[1]

In the post–World War II period, the question has come down to the degree of freedom the President should have in formulating national interests, particularly vital interests, not whether he should have the primary role. This was because, after more than a century of debate among constitutional lawyers, the courts and Congress were unwilling clearly to limit the President's authority when there was real danger to the vital interests of the nation. The dilemma is at the heart of American democracy; how can the nation survive in an international environment that was, and still is, strongly influenced by governments that are essentially undemocratic in character unless it gives one branch of government the authority to speak and act for the whole nation? On the other hand, if the President is given broad powers to determine national interests and to conduct foreign policy, how can a democratic society insure that he will not abuse those powers? Paul Seabury has assessed the problem as follows: "A tension developed between these doctrines of separation and limitation of powers and the exigencies of world politics. Domestic constitutionalism restrained power and established checks upon the modes and objects of its employment. A concern for national political and military security could often recommend exactly the opposite. . . . What in a domestic context was a virtue was in an international context a vice."[2]

World War II, and the lessons the American people drew about its origins and the nation's lack of preparation, resulted in a rather dramatic change in executive-legislative relationships concerning the making of foreign policy and in determining national interests. As the United States began in the Truman administration to look beyond the narrow defense needs of the country to the requirements of a stable world order in which American trade and investment could prosper and friendly nations could feel secure from hostile neighbors, the United States gradually assumed the responsibilities of a world power. Although Congress was carefully brought into the discussions that led to such dramatic departures in traditional American foreign policy as the Truman Doctrine, the Marshall Plan, and the North Atlantic Pact, all these initiatives came from the executive branch and were ratified by Congress in the form of legislation or treaty. The perceived danger of international Communism in the early postwar period, when Communist China joined the Soviet Union in an alliance early in 1950, led to even greater power being assumed by the President to determine worldwide national interests. At the outbreak of the Korean War in June 1950, for example, President Truman did not even seek a con-

1 *The Presidency: Office and Powers* (New York, 1957), p. 171.
2 *Power, Freedom and Diplomacy* (New York, 1963), p. 194.

gressional resolution of support, let alone a declaration of war, before he ordered American forces into combat, where they remained for three years. Fifteen years later, when President Johnson sent troops into battle in Vietnam, he could at least point to the overwhelming congressional support for the Tonkin Gulf Resolution of 1964 to justify his action.

By 1969, the American people and Congress once again drew certain conclusions from a war, this time the Vietnam experience,[3] and the Senate began searching for ways to reduce the President's authority to decide vital national interests. Congressional efforts to attach amendments to foreign-aid legislation restricting the President's freedom to conduct the war in Indochina and its other efforts to impose a terminal date for withdrawal of all American forces from Vietnam were evidence of the changed mood of the country. The executive branch sharply opposed congressional efforts to limit the President's authority in making foreign policy. Arguments of the elitist school were clearly voiced, namely, that Congress and the public did not have access to sensitive information about the state of the world and that the President's judgment of what the national interest should be in Indochina ought to prevail. Yet, as Charles O. Lerche concluded in his study of American foreign policy-making, "the argument of the elitists is largely beside the point; the American mass public is not prepared to accede to any verdict of inadequacy brought against it."[4]

The conclusion seems to be that the President still has the primary, but not necessarily the decisive, role in determining what United States national interests should be. But the more important question is, how does he exercise that role, and how does Congress limit his authority when it concludes he has either abused it or blundered in exercising it? In addressing this matter of executive-legislative relationships in assessing national interests, it is important to keep in mind the two roles the President fills: that of chief foreign-policy spokesman of the United States, and that of Commander-in-Chief of the Armed Forces.

[3] A case study on how U.S. interests in Vietnam increased from 1945 to 1965 is found in Ch. 6.

[4] *Foreign Policy of the American People*, 3d ed. (Englewood Cliffs, N.J., 1967), p. 31.

The President as Chief Foreign-Policy Spokesman

In the conduct of foreign relations, the Constitution gives the President a clear mandate by vesting in him the powers to conclude treaties, subject to Senate ratification; appoint and receive ambassadors; and communicate with foreign governments. Corwin concluded that "the President has all powers that the facts of international intercourse may at any time make conveniently applicable if the Constitution does not vest them elsewhere in clear terms. Ordinarily, this means that the initiative in the foreign field rests with him."[5] The President today has access to an enormous amount of information about the state of the international environment which is not normally available to the public and to Congress and he therefore has a clear advantage in anticipating crises abroad that may affect national interests. Also, the President has the vast resources of the federal bureaucracy at his disposal to analyze events abroad and formulate policies to deal with them. But the formulation of policies to deal with the changing international environment is not the same as deciding the extent to which the United States ought to be involved, i.e., the intensity of the national interest. This function often is performed by only a handful of men in the executive branch, sometimes by the President alone.

Traditionally, the State Department has been the primary government agency involved in the conduct of United States foreign policy, but it is not always the primary adviser of the President in the assessment of national interests or the formulation of foreign policy. In Franklin Roosevelt's administration, the State Department was only peripherally involved in foreign policy making, but under Truman and Eisenhower it was heavily involved because there were strong Secretaries of State who had the full confidence of the President, namely, Marshall and Acheson under Truman, and Dulles under Eisenhower. In the Kennedy administration, the Defense Department headed by Robert McNamara overshadowed the State Department in formulating foreign policy, whereas in the Johnson administration Secretary of State Rusk came to exercise the primary influence. The Cen-

[5] Corwin, *The Presidency*, p. 180.

tral Intelligence Agency (CIA), set up in 1948, had a large influence on the formulation of foreign policy in the 1950's because of its brilliant director, Allen Dulles; however, the CIA declined in influence following the disastrous Bay of Pigs operation in Cuba in 1961, which it had planned and executed with knowledge of Presidents Eisenhower and Kennedy. In the first Nixon administration, foreign policy making as well as the formulation of United States national interests was, to a large extent, moved out of both the State Department and the Pentagon and put into the White House under the leadership of the President's Assistant for National Security Affairs Henry Kissinger. The President's use of Kissinger to negotiate secretly with Chinese and North Vietnamese leaders in 1971 and 1972 was further evidence of his desire to run foreign policy from the White House, not the State Department. This shift of power has caused considerable frustration both among Foreign Service officers and some Defense Department elements, but it is indicative of the fact that the President, not the executive agencies, has the responsibility to determine how policy shall be formulated.

In formulating the national defense interests of the United States, the President relies primarily on the National Security Council (NSC) for advice from within the executive branch. The NSC, established by the National Security Act of 1947, has as its statutory members the President, Vice President, Secretary of State, Secretary of Defense, and Director of the Office of Emergency Preparedness. By custom, the Director of Central Intelligence and the Chairman of the Joint Chiefs of Staff are usually invited by the President to attend. The President's Assistant for National Security Affairs almost always attends. Depending on the issues to be addressed, the President may ask the Director of the Office of Management and Budget to attend. In the Kennedy and first Nixon administrations, the Attorney General was a regular participant at NSC meetings. This small group of men has the large responsibility of advising the President on the actions he should take to deal with foreign threats to the defense of the United States, as well as foreign events that could have a significant effect on the stability of the international environment, on which American security rests. Implicit in the advice they render the President is their perception of national interests in various parts of the world and how a failure to act might be interpreted by potential enemies and friends.

Each of these key advisers perceives the national interest from a somewhat different perspective: The Secretary of State is deeply interested in how other governments will react to United States policy moves; the Secretary of Defense and the Chairman of the Joint Chiefs of Staff are concerned about a potential enemy's capabilities to harm the United States or its allies; the Director of Central Intelligence is concerned with a potential enemy's intentions and intrigues; the Vice President and the Attorney General have an appreciation of the legal and congressional aspects of a foreign policy decision, as well as a feeling for how the public may react; the Director of Emergency Preparedness is involved in seeing that the nation is prepared internally to fight a war if necessary; and the President's National Security Adviser seeks to insure that all options and arguments have had a fair hearing. But the important factor is that the President alone makes the final decision. Normally, he does not decide in the presence of his subordinates but informs them of his decision in writing through his Assistant for National Security Affairs. The President usually consults with individuals outside the executive departments and agencies, congressional leaders, and private citizens whose judgment he values. But an essential ingredient in all decisions involving national defense and international security interests is full and accurate information about the problem the nation faces; for this information he relies heavily on the various intelligence agencies of government, whose products are funneled to the President primarily by the Director of Central Intelligence, and also by the Assistant to the President for National Security Affairs.[6]

When the President deals with problems affecting the economic interests of the country, he uses a somewhat different set of advisers, for example, the Secretary of Treasury, Secretary of Commerce, the Secretary of State and perhaps his Council of Economic Advisers. This is because he will be dealing with prob-

---

[6] The reconnaissance information provided by CIA just prior to the Cuban Missile Crisis in 1962 is an excellent example.

lems that have to do primarily with the United States economy and the well-being of American enterprise operating in the international sphere. Here he deals with balance-of-payments problems and terms of trade, with exchange rates and trade restrictions against United States goods. In the Nixon administration there was established in the White House for the first time a coordinating office whose function is similar in the economic field to that of the NSC staff in the national security field. Named the Council on International Economic Policy, it is headed by a presidential assistant who serves as coordinator of the various offices in the executive agencies that are involved in international economic affairs, including the State Department.[7]

It is not the purpose here to elaborate on the roles of the agencies involved in formulating policies in support of United States economic interests, but rather to indicate that the advice the President receives from these subordinates may differ from the counsel he gets from his National Security Council. This is because in the field of trade and commerce his advisers are concerned primarily with the interests of American business and labor, with the strength of the national economy, and with the soundness of the dollar in international financial markets. To some degree, economic and trade advisers may take a more parochial view of national interests because they are in contact with many private-interest groups within the United States who may not be impressed with the necessity of harming certain United States enterprises for the sake of more world free trade. Advisers concerned primarily with the United States economy and private business are not as convinced as some military leaders of the necessity of maintaining bases in many parts of the world, which create a drain on the balance of payments. Neither are they sympathetic with some State Department officials who wish to maintain good relations with key allies even at the expense of hurting some American business interests. Japan is an example: United States aid built up Japanese industry in the 1950's and 1960's to the point where it was able to compete suc-

---

[7] The first presidential assistant in this position, Peter Peterson, became Secretary of Commerce in 1972. He was succeeded by Peter Flanigan, who continued to hold this position in the second Nixon administration.

cessfully with American producers in many foreign countries and even in the United States; but the United States continued to carry the main defense burden in Japan and did little until 1971 to force Japan to recognize the necessity of adopting a new exchange rate for the yen and lifting import restrictions on certain American products.[8]

By the summer of 1971 the United States' international economic position had become so serious that President Nixon took bold actions to defend the national economic interest. His principal adviser and spokesman in this effort was Secretary of the Treasury John Connally, who pressured European and Japanese leaders to help improve the United States balance-of-payments position. His forceful methods caused some concern among America's allies and friends, but this represented a dramatic example of the President's deciding that vital economic interests were at stake and that they should take precedence over the feelings, and perhaps even friendship, of some of this nation's allies. Some critics believed that the President's strong actions had a harmful effect on United States–Japanese relations, which could affect American defense interests in the future; on the other hand, supporters of the President's moves believed that he was being realistic about United States interests in a changing world economic environment in which it would have to compete more vigorously with other industrial powers to maintain its trading position, and perhaps also its economic well-being. The New Economic Policy of 1971, therefore, represented a victory for those within government and in the country at large who had been arguing that America's economic position was being seriously eroded during the 1960's because of an overriding concern with national defense; they urged on the President the view that if the nation expected to play a major world role in the future, he had to put its economic house in order, even if this harmed American relations with some friendly countries.

[8] The cleavage within the Nixon administration on this issue was dramatized in the summer of 1970 when the Assistant Secretary of Commerce for International Affairs was forced to resign because of differences with the White House over trade policy toward Japan. A year later, President Nixon took a much stronger stand against Japan on trade matters, to the regret of some elements of the State Department.

In dealing with the third basic national interest – world peace and order – the President relies on the National Security Council for advice, but he also brings into his circle of advisers the United States Ambassador to the United Nations, the Director of the Arms Control and Disarmament Agency, and sometimes roving ambassadors whose function is to seek ways of reaching understandings with other nations to avoid conflicts that might lead to war and to stop those already in progress. To a very large extent, the President relies on diplomacy to carry out all these policies, but the determination of the degree of interest involved usually is made after he consults with his National Security Council.

The emphasis the President gives to international efforts to build world peace and order depends to a large degree on his and the nation's perception of the threat to national defense and economic interests at any given time. For example, in the early post–World War II period, President Truman gave much support to United Nations efforts to settle international disputes through peaceful means, and he permitted a large degree of disarmament to take place within the United States. When his perception of Soviet intentions turned in the late 1940's from optimism to alarm, particularly after the outbreak of the Korean War, he put less emphasis on trying to reach understandings through the United Nations and instead began to build up the United States alliance system and greatly increased the nation's armed strength. All postwar presidents have given support to United Nations disarmament efforts, but it was in the 1960's, after the Cuban Missile Crisis, that President Kennedy and President Johnson were able to obtain agreements with the Soviet Union on limiting the atmospheric testing of nuclear weapons and a nuclear nonproliferation treaty with other nations. Both Presidents Johnson and Nixon gave strong support to efforts to reach an arms limitation agreement with the Soviet Union, and in May 1972 these efforts finally bore fruit when President Nixon visited Moscow and signed a SALT agreement.

Support for the United Nations as a peace-keeping organization has not improved measurably, however, since the late 1940's, even though each President has given lip service to the organization and several have appointed distinguished representatives to the international organization.[9] Popular support for the United Nations in the United States, and perhaps official support as well, probably reached its lowest ebb in the fall of 1971 when the General Assembly voted to oust the Republic of China (Taiwan) from its midst and to substitute a Peking delegation. This was seen as a significant diplomatic reverse for the United States, but from the President's view of longer-term national interests, it probably was a necessary price to pay for an improvement of United States relations with the People's Republic of China. One reason that Nixon may have taken this bold action was his perception that the world political climate was ripe for negotiations to strengthen world peace and order.

The President as Commander-in-Chief

Although the framers of the Constitution were careful to give Congress the power to declare war and to raise armies, they were not willing to tie the President's hands in dealing with foreign dangers. They were aware that the world of power politics into which the new nation was embarked required that the chief executive be given sufficient flexibility in the use of the armed forces so that the nation's interests would not be placed in jeopardy because of his inability to act in case of an imminent danger. The Constitution sought to take care of both possibilities by giving Congress the right to declare war and the President the powers of Commander-in-Chief to make war. The Constitution did not specify whether the President could employ the armed forces outside the United States without a declaration of war from the Congress, but it has generally been accepted by the courts that the President may use the armed forces to enforce the law, part of which is international law, and to protect the rights of American citizens abroad. As Corwin points out: "dozens and scores of episodes have occurred in our history in which Presidents have done this very thing [used armed forces abroad

9 Henry Cabot Lodge in the Eisenhower administration and Adlai Stevenson in the Kennedy and Johnson administrations were outstanding public servants who had direct access to the President in carrying out their roles at the United Nations.

without authorization from Congress] and have been defended by their champions with the argument that when action of this sort is in defense of what international law itself recognizes as rights of person and property and is not excessive, it is not an act of war or a legitimate cause for warlike retort by the country suffering from it." [10]

If the President may use armed forces to protect American legal rights abroad, is he permitted to use them also to protect American interests, as he defines them? Hamilton and Jefferson debated this issue in 1801 when American vessels were being attacked by ships of the Bey of Tripoli. Jefferson argued that American ships had the right only of self-defense, unless Congress formally declared war; Hamilton contended that, even though the Constitution clearly meant that only Congress had the authority to take the nation into war, if war were forced on the United States by hostile acts of another nation the United States was already at war and the President could act accordingly. [11] This dilemma of what is a war, what is a police action, and what are the President's prerogatives in using armed force short of major conflict is one that has been debated throughout American history.

The opinions of the courts and the reactions of Congress over the years give the President wide latitude in using the armed forces when the risks of a large war are not great, particularly when the area of action is in geographic proximity to American borders. Historically, Presidents have had wider freedom in using the navy abroad than the army, one reason being that the navy, with marines embarked, is more capable of limited engagements with hostile forces than is the army, with its logistic requirements and, usually, its larger manpower. But there are no clearly defined guidelines to tell a President when a police action is likely to become a war and when he should obtain congressional approval for his action. In the final analysis, this becomes a matter of political judgment on the part of the President. Some Presidents, such as McKinley and Eisenhower, have been

---

[10] Corwin, *The Presidency*, p. 198. See also Arthur Schlesinger, Jr., "Congress and the Making of American Foreign Policy," *Foreign Affairs*, October 1972, pp. 78–113, for a detailed discussion of this issue.

[11] Ibid., p. 199.

cautious in using armed force without the consent of Congress, while others, like Theodore Roosevelt and Truman, have used the armed forces in a way they believed would be supported by the American people, and they often ignored Congress. Franklin Roosevelt was very cautious about using the armed forces in a provocative way until 1940, when Europe was at war and the American people were slowly coming to realize that their own security was in danger if Hitler conquered all of Europe.

The prime factor probably is the President's judgment of whether congressional approval of his military actions will be helpful in prosecuting whatever role he envisages for the armed forces. If the survival of the nation may be at stake – for example, the Cuban Missile Crisis – or when the nation is attacked in a flagrant manner, as at Pearl Harbor, a President hardly needs a declaration of war because the people can be expected to rally to his support in time of grave danger. But when the danger is not close to American territory and if the public does not perceive a vital national interest to be at stake, the President may find it prudent politics to obtain at least a resolution of support from Congress, if not a declaration of war, before he employs sizable military forces to protect what he believes to be vital to the nation. President Eisenhower, for example, insisted on obtaining congressional consent for his actions in the Taiwan Strait Crisis in 1955 and in the Middle East in 1958; President Truman, on the other hand, did not ask Congress for approval of his actions in Korea. Good politics usually will convince the President that he should at least consult with Congress before engaging in major hostilities, as he is dependent on congressional support for any funds he may need to carry out the military action and for authorizing increases in the size of the armed forces. Some Presidents have confronted the Congress with a *fait accompli* on the assumption that it would never refuse to provide the wherewithal to prosecute a war once United States forces were engaged, but he must then weigh the risks of such a course if his actions may later become so unpopular that Congress blames him for having taken them. The advantage in obtaining a resolution of Congress for the use of armed force is that responsibility for the action then is shared between the executive and legislative branches of government, and because it probably will have greater legitimacy with the public if the cost or duration of the conflict proves to be greater than the public originally was prepared to accept.

In the final analysis, the President's role as Commander-in-Chief is likely to be judged less by the legalities of his exercise of power than by the wisdom with which he uses the power at his disposal. If he wisely perceives the national interest and uses military power sparingly in defense of it, he is likely to be acclaimed a great leader. If he does not use his military power wisely, no amount of consultation with Congress and adherence to a strict legal interpretation of his powers will save him from rebuke. In sum, it is imperative that the President be a sufficiently wise politician to perceive correctly the national interest in terms that are acceptable to the electorate and be a forceful enough Commander-in-Chief to use military power in a way that will contain rather than enlarge conflicts abroad.

Congress as the Balance Wheel in Formulating National Interests

If Congress is precluded by constitutional interpretation from exercising primary leadership in foreign affairs and in determining the precise nature of United States national interests, it clearly has great influence in setting the boundaries within which the President formulates his concept of national interests. The Constitution specifically gives to the Senate authority to approve treaties concluded by the President, and it also gives the Senate authority to confirm the appointment of ambassadors abroad. The Constitution does not, however, give the Senate authority to decide on recognition of foreign governments and on the acceptance of foreign ambassadors. This is solely the President's responsibility. But even more important than these specific grants of authority in foreign affairs, the Congress exercises great influence on the formulation of national interests through its legislative power – as most foreign-policy measures require implementing legislation – and through the power of the purse. The power of Congress to investigate any areas which require legislation carries with it considerable latitude to question the

President's perception of the national interest, as well as the policies he chooses to advance. Congress is the public sounding board for policies initiated by the executive branch, and it is here that it probably serves its most important role in the foreign-policy field: a check on presidential initiatives.

By providing for checks and balances on presidential power, the Constitutional Convention envisaged that both the President and Congress would be involved in determining what the national interest should be at any given time and place, at least in the broad guidelines.

How, then, has this division of responsibility worked in practice? American history shows that there has been little consistency in this regard. Those chief executives who believed with Hamilton that the President has inherent powers to do whatever he deems necessary, unless the Constitution specifically gives such powers to Congress, have exercised considerable freedom in formulating national interests – often ignoring Congress or proceeding on the assumption that if the President takes decisive action Congress probably will support his view. Other Presidents, taking their cue from Madison and adopting a stricter construction of the meaning of the Constitution, have not acted forcefully until or unless they thought they had the support of Congress for their actions. Theodore Roosevelt was an example of the former type, and Dwight Eisenhower was an adherent of the latter view.

Since the turn of the century, when the United States assumed a larger role in the world, the trend has been toward stronger presidential leadership in formulating the national interest. However, during both world wars, President Wilson and President Franklin Roosevelt moved cautiously toward hardening United States policy vis-à-vis Germany and Japan (in World War II) because there was deep opposition within the country, and in Congress, to the idea that the United States had a vital interest in the outcome of those struggles for power. Only after public opinion became sufficiently aroused by German victories and threats to United States shipping did the two Presidents move the nation toward war.[12]

[12] The turning point for Franklin Roosevelt seemed to be congressional pas-

The period since World War II has brought both an era of considerable cooperation between the chief executive and Congress in the formulation of national interests and, in the late 1960's, a serious erosion of the role of Congress – particularly the Senate. In his memoirs former Secretary of State Dean Acheson outlined in considerable detail[13] the process of "non-partisanship" in foreign policy that prevailed during the Truman administration with a Republican-controlled Senate. This was a period in which the United States vastly expanded its interests throughout the world and took on treaty commitments in Europe and in Latin America designed to contain Soviet power and influence. The Marshall Plan, one of the most far-reaching foreign ventures ever undertaken by one nation in behalf of others, was enacted less than ten years after Congress roundly criticized President Roosevelt for giving fifty old destroyers to Britain to help her survive. Similarly, during the Eisenhower administration, a Democratic-controlled Congress cooperated on most major foreign-policy issues, including the Southeast Asia Defense Treaty and the joint resolutions in support of presidential policies in Taiwan and the Middle East. But even in the 1950's, Congress gradually relinquished some authority in the formulation of national interests because it gave broad grants of power to the President to use his own judgment on the deployment of the armed forces. President Truman did not ask for a congressional resolution of support for his military actions in Korea, preferring to rely on United States obligations under the United Nations Charter for legal justification of his actions.

In the 1960's, particularly after United States military intervention in Vietnam in 1965, cooperation between the President and the Senate Foreign Relations Committee began to disintegrate. When that committee took an increasingly critical view of Vietnam policy in 1966 and 1967, the Johnson administration bypassed it and relied instead on the Senate Armed Services Committee, which was more cooperative in supporting the President's war effort. In 1970, however the Foreign Relations Com-

---

sage of the Lend-Lease Act in the spring of 1941. Thereafter, he adopted a much more provocative policy toward Germany and Japan.

[13] *Present at the Creation* (New York, 1969), Ch. 12.

mittee reasserted its influence in defining United States interests in Southeast Asia by unanimously endorsing the Cooper-Church Amendment to the military assistance legislation; this was designed to restrict the President's use of military forces in Cambodia. The amendment carried in the full Senate and was hailed by its backers as a sign that the Senate had finally restored some balance between it and the chief executive in the foreign-policy field.[14]

The contest between the Senate and the President to determine the limits of United States national interests abroad has nowhere been better illustrated than in the running debate that took place between the Foreign Relations Committee and the State Department from 1967 to 1969 on Senate Resolution 85, better known as the Resolution on National Commitments. This resolution, put before the Senate in April 1969, read as follows: "Whereas accurate definition of the term 'national commitment' in recent years has become obscured: Now, therefore, be it resolved, That it is the sense of the Senate that a national commitment by the United States to a foreign power necessarily and exclusively results from affirmative action taken by the executive and legislative branches of the United States Government through means of a treaty, convention, or other legislative instrumentality specifically intended to give effect to such a commitment."[15] The committee sought to establish through extensive hearings and discussion the principle that the President does not have authority to commit the United States to defend a foreign nation unless Congress in some way gives its assent to such an agreement. The view of the committee was summed up as follows: "the committee believes that the restoration of constitutional balance in the making of foreign commitments is not only compatible with the requirements of efficiency but essential to the purposes of democracy." Taking issue with Undersecretary of State Nicholas Katzenbach's view "that the demarcation of authority between President and Congress can and should be left

---

[14] This claim was made even though it was doubtful whether the House of Representatives, which has been more favorable to the President's foreign policies, would agree to this specific limitation on presidential powers in foreign relations.

[15] U.S., Congress, Senate, *National Commitments: Senate Report No. 91–129*, 91st Cong., 1st sess., 16 April 1969.

to be settled 'by the instinct of the nation and its leaders for political responsibility,' " the committee asserted, "The Framers of
the Constitution gave us more specific and reliable guidelines for
drawing the line of demarcation, particularly as to treaty making
and the authority to commit the country to war." [16] The committee placed a major share of the blame for the erosion of congressional authority in foreign affairs squarely on its own shoulders:
"Both the executive and the Congress have been periodically un-
mindful of constitutional requirements and proscriptions, the
executive by its incursions upon Congressional prerogative at
moments when action seemed more important than the means of
its initiation, the Congress by its uncritical and sometimes un-
conscious acquiescence in these incursions. If blame is to be ap-
portioned, a fair share belongs to the Congress." [17] Recounting
the instances, beginning with Roosevelt's exchange of destroyers
for British bases in 1940, where the chief executive greatly expanded his use of the armed forces without obtaining congressional authority, and with special attention given to the Tonkin
Gulf Resolution of 1964, the committee's report asserted that the
intention of the commitments resolution was "an invitation to
the executive to reconsider its excesses, and to the legislature to
reconsider its omissions, in the making of foreign policy, and, in
the light of such reconsideration, to bring their foreign policy
practices back into compliance with that division of responsibility envisioned by the Constitution and sanctioned by over a
century of usage." [18] Finally, the committee recommended the following four steps to accomplish this objective in considering future resolutions involving the use, or possible use, of the armed
forces:

1) Debate the proposed resolution at sufficient length to establish a legislative record showing the intent of Congress; 2) Use the words "authorize" or
"empower" or such other language as will leave no doubt that Congress
alone has the right to authorize the initiation of war and that, in granting
the President authority to use the armed forces, Congress is granting him
power that he would not otherwise have; 3) State in the resolution, as explicitly as possible under the circumstances, the kind of military action that

[16] Ibid., pp. 9–10.
[17] Ibid., pp. 7–8.
[18] Ibid., p. 80.

is being authorized and the place and purpose of its use; and 4) Put a time limit on the resolution, thereby assuring Congress the opportunity to review its decision and extend or terminate the President's authority to use military force.

The view of the executive branch regarding Senate Resolution 85 was contained in a letter dated March 10, 1969, from Assistant Secretary of State William Macomber to Senator J. William Fulbright, Chairman of the Foreign Relations Committee. Asserting that the legislative and executive branches had worked well together in the past, the State Department concluded that problems which arise concerning the extent of consultation and consent of Congress in foreign affairs could be more effectively dealt with through better procedures for consultation, rather than through Senate Resolution 85 which would not, the State Department contended, change the constitutional powers of the President. "In our view Senate Resolution 85 would tend to detract from efforts at cooperation between the two branches by focusing attention on a statement of policy that does not accurately reflect the constitutional balance between the executive and legislative branches." [19]

The only dissenting member of the Foreign Relations Committee to the report on national commitments was Senator Gale McGee, who wrote a strong minority report. Starting with the assertion that the resolution was an "ill-advised way in which to seek to achieve some sort of balance in foreign policy matters," McGee cited America's sudden emergence as the most powerful nation in the world and also the advent of the nuclear age to support his view that "the authority to make decisions and take action supporting them must be located in one place. From the rather meager beginnings of our constitutional system when Congress shared more directly with the President some of the policy processes, we have now come to an age when the pressure of time and the multiplicity of other issues scarcely allow the Congress more than a passing glance at some of the most important decisions in the history of mankind." Citing the fact that the Constitution gives the President alone the authority to recognize

[19] Ibid., p. 38.

foreign governments and to enter into commitments that implement that recognition, the Senator argued that the President necessarily must have the power to make many commitments to foreign governments. He also argued that, as Commander-in-Chief of the armed forces, "the President has the constitutional power to send U. S. military forces abroad when he deems it to be in the national interest." Charging that the proposed Senate resolution "implies that the President and the Congress together would be the exclusive means by which the Government of the United States in the future could enter into commitments with a foreign power, it runs counter to constitutional intent." Admitting that there were some risks involved in granting to the President increasing power in the field of foreign affairs, Senator McGee argued that "there would appear to be no reasonable alternative to assuming those risks save at the price of confusion, delay and even inaction through some series of yet unspecified procedures implied in the commitments resolution. . . . To have to revert to Senate debate and discussion at a time like that would be cumbersome at the very least and disastrous to the national interest in the extreme."[20]

It is of interest that former Undersecretary of State Katzenbach, who had strongly defended the President's authority to send large American forces to Vietnam when he testified before the Foreign Relations Committee in 1967, urged Congress as a private citizen in 1970 to assert its political power to restrain presidential authority in foreign affairs. He agreed with the Cooper-Church Amendment to the foreign aid legislation (restricting funds from being used in Cambodia) and urged Congress to "use political power in specific and meaningful ways." Asserting that the President has vast powers in using the armed forces overseas "if he can get away with it politically," he suggested that Congress's most effective role is to convince the President that if he makes certain kinds of commitments to foreign countries, he will not have the support of Congress.[21] Thus, the Johnson administration's expert on the legal aspects of presiden-

[20] U.S., Congress, Senate, Committee on Foreign Relations, *United States Commitments to Foreign Powers: Hearing,* 90th Cong., 1st sess., 1967, pp. 71–110.
[21] *Washington Post,* July 19, 1970.

tial powers in foreign affairs supported the view of constitu-
tionalists such as Edwin Corwin that the only effective restraint
on the President's authority in the foreign field is political rather
than legal power. Senator Fulbright, who obviously regretted
granting the President such wide legal authority in the Tonkin
Gulf Resolution of 1964, exerted great efforts from 1967 onward
to use the power of the purse, plus the powers of congressional
investigation, to convince the President it would be politically
unwise for him to make new foreign-policy commitments or to
use the armed forces in any significant way abroad without con-
sulting and obtaining the assent of the Senate.[22]

What should be the proper role of Congress, then, in determining the national interests of the United States? It seems clear
that in the nuclear age when the peace and freedom of millions
of people may hinge on the American President's ability to act
quickly in case of crisis – when a survival interest of the United
States and its allies is clearly at stake – the President should not
be deprived of freedom of action by a Senate whose delay in
giving advice and consent could bring disaster to the nation. But
the real question is the degree to which Congress should be involved in deciding national interests when the danger is not
immediate, but when major and vital interests may be affected.
The constitutional fathers clearly did not intend that the President should have unlimited powers to determine United States
foreign policy, or commit the nation to war; the Congress, in
particular the Senate, was given the role of watchdog over the
executive branch to serve as a check on actions and decisions it
might consider unwise. Although Congress did relinquish some
of its responsibilities as balance wheel in formulating national
interests during the 1950's and 1960's by granting the President
more freedom to use the armed forces in Asia and the Middle
East than was, in retrospect, prudent, an important reason was
that during an era of bipartisanship Congress did not feel much
risk in giving the President resolutions of support because there
seemed to be a national consensus on major foreign-policy ob-

---

22 President Nixon's strong opposition to the Cooper-Church Amendment to
the foreign aid legislation in 1970 and 1971 was evidence that he too opposed any
infringement on his powers to conduct U.S. foreign policy.

jectives. Another factor may have been that such delays of support for presidential authority seemed to succeed in convincing
potential enemies that the United States was prepared to take
military action if necessary to support its interests. However, the
costs of the Vietnam War turned out to be much greater than
Congress ever anticipated so that a reexamination of the national
interest was demanded by the Foreign Relations Committee.

Thus, the Senate in 1970–1972 made strenuous efforts to re-
establish certain limits on presidential authority in the foreign-
policy field, but in the final analysis these bounds probably
would turn out to be political rather than legal ones. The watchdog role can be played by giving the President an admonition
that will have the effect of causing him anguish when he or
his political party faces the electorate or when he needs funds
to carry out policies. Under this situation, the President would
still have great latitude in determining the national interest in
time of crisis, but he would be on notice that he might have to
pay a large political price if he perceives the national interest in a
radically different way from that prevailing in the Congress and
among the American people.

The President and the Isolation of the Presidency

This discussion of the President's and Congress's role in formulating national interests would not be complete without mention
of what George Reedy has described as the "isolation of the
presidency" from the political realities of this country. In his
book *The Twilight of the Presidency,* Reedy argues that no matter how skillful a politician a man has been when he is elected
President, the nature of the office today cuts him off from the
face-to-face criticisms that take place in Congress and elsewhere
in American politics; this increases the likelihood that the President will commit political blunders out of ignorance of the
political climate in the country and in Congress.[23] Even the
Senate (which Reedy describes as a great example of adversary

---

[23] See Reedy's description of the ways in which a president is transformed into
a monarch figure after he is inaugurated and is settled in the White House; Ch.
1, "The American Monarchy" (New York, 1970).

relationships where members are "extremely strong-minded men who do not hesitate to express their opinion of each other in basic English") does not normally provide the kind of direct confrontation for a President that Reedy believes is a necessity if he is to avoid mistakes in foreign and domestic policy through miscalculation. He contends that "Senators do not play the role of adversary in the presence of the chief executive. This is not because entry into the portals of the White House taps previously unrealized reserves of diffidence. It is simply that they have found it inadvisable to be anything other than respectful. The aura of reverence that surrounds the President when he is in the Mansion is so universal that the slightest hint of criticism automatically labels a man as a colossal lout."[24] Reedy does not argue that individual senators fail to criticize the President and his policies, but rather that they fail to do so in face-to-face confrontations with the chief executive. A Senator Morse or Fulbright[25] or Mc-Govern may sharply challenge his judgment in foreign affairs, but Reedy maintains that such criticism is rarely heard in the Oval Room or the Cabinet Room of the White House when senators are called in for consultation. Robert Kennedy made a similar point in describing the debate that went on in the Kennedy administration over the handling of the Cuban Missile Crisis.[26]

In addition to the constitutional question about how much independence the President should have in conducting foreign affairs and in deploying the armed forces, there is this disturbing question about the President's political awareness of what is going on in the United States and how this lack of awareness may affect his perception of the nation's total interests at any given time. Some argue that domestic political considerations should not be part of the process of determining the nation's vital interests – that "the President knows best" what the nation needs to do to protect itself. However, given the nature of the American political system, a prudent President usually will carefully assess

24 Ibid., p. 80.
25 Fulbright's book *Arrogance of Power*, published in 1966, was a powerful attack on President Johnson's perception of U.S. national interests, particularly in Southeast Asia, and it received wide attention among the educated elites.
26 Robert Kennedy, *The Thirteen Days* (New York, 1969).

the mood of the nation before he embarks on a foreign-policy course that runs a high risk of being rejected by the electorate. Occasionally, the President must take certain risks in foreign affairs and hope that the electorate will accept his judgment after the facts are fully known,[27] but this is quite different from arguing that the public does not know enough about the state of the world to make a valid judgment about United States vital interests. If the American system of government is to operate effectively in the latter half of the twentieth century, there must continue to be checks and balances on presidential power in foreign as well as in domestic affairs. If a President blunders in his assessment of a domestic problem, his party may be endangered in the next election; but if he blunders in the international arena because he does not have public support when his policies reach a critical point, the consequences of such a miscalculation can be extremely serious for the whole nation. President Kennedy's refusal to use United States forces at the height of the Bay of Pigs episode in April 1961 and President Johnson's decision in March 1968 not to send an additional 200,000 troops to Vietnam were cases of the President's realizing his miscalculation about the nation's willingness to accept his perception of the national interest. In both cases, the United States paid a considerable price in terms of international prestige for having embarked on a policy it could not sustain at a critical point. Had the President in either case consulted fully with congressional leaders – both supporters and critics – before involving the nation so deeply in a risky course of action, he would at least have been more aware of the political price to be paid if he continued that course. This is not to argue that either President would have changed his policies earlier had he been confronted by his critics with the hard domestic political realities; but in such a case, the President would have proceeded in full knowledge of the possible political consequences of his actions, rather than in ignorance of them.

[27] President Nixon took such a risk in April–May 1970 when he decided to send U.S. forces into Cambodia for two months to support a South Vietnamese attack on North Vietnamese strongholds there.

4

Roles of Private Interest Groups and Mass Media

ASSESSING the influence of private organizations and opinion leaders in the formulation of national interests is far more difficult than studying the constitutional responsibilities of the President and Congress. James Rosenau, in his study *Public Opinion and Foreign Policy,* draws a distinction between what he calls the "flow of influence" and the "flow of opinion." He points out that scholars have had considerable difficulty in assessing the amount of influence individuals and groups have on policy formulation because of the problems involved in trying to measure such influence.[1] Yet few observers doubt that the influence of the public on major foreign-policy issues is increasing. The reasons are not difficult to find: one, a far larger number of young people are going to college than previously, asking more hard questions about the direction of United States foreign policy, and demanding to be heard; two, mass communications, particularly television, have made it possible for nearly every household in the United States to see and hear the issues of America's role in the world debated and analyzed; and three, more Americans have lived and traveled abroad than ever before, and their experiences and impressions of foreign countries cause them to take a far greater interest in such matters as foreign aid, foreign military bases, and the attitudes of foreign peoples toward the United States than was the case thirty years ago. For these and other reasons, the President and Congress do not have the same degree of freedom that the federal government once had in deciding what the nation's interests should be; now, they have a better educated and better informed public that insists on being heard on matters of foreign policy. This is particularly true of questions involving the vital interests of the nation – where United States troops may be sent overseas to fight. This was well illustrated in the student protest movement of the late 1960's and early 1970's, which was strongly opposed to American policy in Vietnam.

Some writers, such as George Kennan and Hans Morgenthau, have held the view that policy-makers should not be influenced by public opinion because the public is fickle and does not consider the long-term implications of foreign-policy decisions. Charles Lerche takes the opposite point of view and argues that "a democratic government like that of the United States is ideologically committed to follow as nearly as it can the dictates of its constituents. This means that the policy-makers cannot confine their attention to the national interest as they perceive it themselves, but must always heed whatever they feel the voice of the people is saying."[2] Lerche points out that the difference between foreign policy making in a democracy and in a dictatorship is that popular influence on decision-makers is taken for granted in a democratic system; he concludes that "officials in the United States, therefore, must cope with the forces of democratic consensus – and normally must operate within its bounds – as they seek to define and apply the national interest in a rapidly changing world."[3]

Gabriel Almond, in his pioneering work *The American People and Foreign Policy*,[4] believes there are inherent limitations in modern society on the capacity of the public to understand the issues and grasp the significance of the most important problems of public policy. However, Almond concludes that the "function of the public in a democratic policy-making process is to set certain policy criteria in the form of widely held values and expectations. It evaluates the results of policies from the point of view of their conformity to these basic values and expectations."[5] If we accept this view, then one might conclude that in formulating the national interests of the United States, the public sets

[1] (New York, 1961), Ch. 2.
[2] *A Foreign Policy of the American People* (Englewood Cliffs, N.J., 1967), p. 27.
[3] Ibid., p. 28.
[4] (New York, 1950).
[5] Ibid., pp. 5–6.

out the broad parameters and policy-makers formulate specific policies within these guidelines.

Nevertheless, certain segments of the public exert more influence in this process than others – even in the deciding of specific policies. It is the purpose here to outline the nature of the influence exerted by the most important interest groups and by individual opinion-makers whose views are listened to by policy-makers.[6] By describing briefly the nature of the influence these groups bring to bear on the President and on members of Congress, we may get a better understanding of the three basic national interests described in Chapter 1 and the degree of interest flowing from them. The role of the mass media is more important in this regard for the influence they exercise on the policy-makers than on the general public. This is so because the media are an important source of influence on the President and provide another check and balance on his perception of national interests.[7]

BUSINESS ORGANIZATIONS

Traditionally, American business groups have had an enormous influence in the formulation of national interests abroad. Until World War II, the nation was not primarily concerned with national defense and security matters, and international trade and investment were usually considered to be the most important foreign-policy objectives. Also, prior to the Franklin Roosevelt administration, the government in Washington, with a few notable exceptions such as Theodore Roosevelt and Woodrow Wilson, was not heavily involved with international affairs, and advancement of American business abroad was therefore the principal reason for maintaining United States diplomatic mis-

[6] I do not seek here to assess the degree of influence these groups and individuals exert, for that is another and highly speculative subject.

[7] Almond lists four foreign-policy elites in his study: political elites (publicly elected, high appointive, and party leaders), administrative elites of the executive branch, the interest elites of private organizations, and the communications elites of press and radio. (Television was still in its infancy when Almond wrote in 1950). In this chapter, we are primarily concerned with the latter two categories, the interest elites and the communications elites.

sions. In fact, prior to World War II, the Commerce Department had a significant role in formulating foreign policy because the interests of American business abroad were considered to be nearly synonymous with the national interest. Only when the United States began to take on the role of world power at the turn of the century with the acquisition of the Philippines and other Pacific islands from the Spanish did matters of power politics and national defense begin to gain some attention as national interests. However, the promotion of American business in foreign countries was only one side of the coin; the other was protection of domestic markets from foreign goods, and the protective tariff legislation of the 1920's and 1930's was clear evidence of the power exercised by domestic business on the government's perception of the national interest.

In the post–World War II period, American business has continued to exercise considerable influence in the formulation of United States policies overseas; but, unlike the prewar period, it has supported an internationalist foreign policy because it has found that such a policy provided large markets for American goods and investment. Until the 1960's, there was no serious threat to the domestic market because much of the world was still recovering from the war.[8] The United States Chamber of Commerce, the Junior Chamber of Commerce, the National Association of Manufacturers, the largest and most influential of the business organizations, have to one degree or another supported free trade abroad and economic assistance to other nations. The business community favored the Kennedy Round of tariff reductions in the 1960's and other American efforts at international cooperation in trade; this liberal view of international economic relations characterized United States business for about twenty-five years after World War II. But the question must be raised whether this view would have continued to predominate

[8] While German and Japanese cars and electronic equipment were beginning to cause serious competition in the American market, the threat of foreign competition did not affect so wide a spectrum of American industries as to cause a serious problem for the government. By the end of the 1960's, however, protectionist sentiment in Congress was rising, as an increasing number of American business interests were threatened by foreign imports, textiles being the most notable case in point.

had there been a serious downturn in the economy, and had foreign goods replaced American goods in foreign markets and encroached on the American market. American business benefited handsomely in the postwar period from an internationalist view of national interests and was willing to support an American military presence in many parts of the world as being good for American business; however, if building up industrial competitors such as Germany and Japan now results in declining markets for United States goods abroad, and fewer jobs for American workers at home, many business interests concerned primarily with foreign markets and investments may find that firms dealing primarily with domestic markets have gained the ascendancy in the halls of Congress and in the executive branch.

Although it is common to speak of American business interests as influencing the executive departments and Congress through national organizations such as those mentioned above, one cannot overlook the great influence exercised by several huge corporations whose economic power and worldwide operations put them in a class by themselves within the business community. The most notable of these are General Motors Corporation, Ford Motor Company, American Telephone and Telegraph Corporation, International Business Machines, and the principal American oil companies — Standard Oil of New Jersey, Gulf Oil, Aramco. Powerful corporations such as these need no national organization to represent them in Washington; they maintain their own staffs there and work directly with the State Department, the Commerce Department, and members of Congress to insure the protection of their overseas interests. Oil politics receives publicity from time to time when issues arise involving import quotas for foreign oil, or when nationalization of American oil concessions by foreign countries is threatened. Normally these large corporations work quietly behind the scenes in Washington and eschew publicity, but their view of the national interest is listened to in the highest circles of government where key decisions regarding United States policy are made. It is no accident that foreign-aid legislation contains mandatory language cutting off aid to any country that nationalizes United States property without satisfactory compensation.[9] These huge American corporations do not exercise equal influence on the determination of the national interest in every part of the world; but in those areas where their own vital private interests are involved – oil in the Middle East, for example – they are able to bring great influence to bear on policy-makers and on congressmen because of their importance in the major financial circles of this country, their role in balance-of-payments considerations, and also because of their heavy contributions to the political campaigns of congressmen and senators. As Rosenau rightly points out, the amount of influence exercised by such private interests is difficult to measure, but the fact that they do exercise great influence, and in some cases decisive influence, on national policy-makers is not in question.[10]

LABOR ORGANIZATIONS

Labor organizations are less influential in affecting national interests than are business interests, principally because their constituency is more concerned with domestic affairs – wages, prices, pensions – than is the constituency of business, whose stockholders are interested in profits from both foreign and domestic investments. Nevertheless, American labor does have a stake in opening up and maintaining foreign markets for American products if these stimulate employment. Conversely, labor organizations may be the first to bring pressure on Congress and the administration when a shutdown of an industry occurs because of a growing influx of cheap foreign products. One reason that

[9] It is also no accident that half of all foreign aid shipped abroad must be in U.S. ships, even though the cost of using U.S. ships may be several times higher than foreign ships.

[10] In August 1970 President Nixon announced, after long study within his administration, that he would not alter the quota system on imports of oil, despite strong political pressures from the New England states and representatives of other interests. If he had agreed to larger imports of cheaper Mid-East oil, as had been proposed, there is no doubt that certain American oil interests would have suffered financially even though the public might have paid less for oil and gasoline. By 1972, however, it was clear that the nation's growing energy needs would require larger oil imports and this fact would have an important effect on perception of national interests in the coming decade, particularly in the Middle East.

the two largest labor organizations, the CIO and the AFL, supported free trade and an internationalist foreign policy after World War II is that these policies seemed to benefit the workingman through a rise in his standard of living, made possible in part by expanding overseas markets for American goods. So long as unemployment remained low, American labor did not seriously question free-trade policies that resulted in the reduction of the labor force in some industries. Yet, protectionist sentiment is now at least as strong in labor groups as in some sectors of the business community; any serious reduction in jobs resulting from foreign competition, especially if this comes during a recessionary period in the economy when there is little expansion in the export industries, could bring about a coalition of labor and business groups working toward congressional enactment of protective legislation. Such a coalition of domestic-oriented business and labor organizations appeared to be gathering momentum in the early 1970's as more members of Congress voiced support for protective measures against certain Japanese imports. The Burke-Hartke bill before Congress in 1972 was the most dramatic proposal to protect American jobs against foreign competition.

The American labor movement has exercised another influence on the national interest in the period since 1949, when the Cold War with the Soviet Union began in earnest. American labor, particularly after the CIO successfully ousted the leaders of several Communist-oriented unions, became strongly anti-Communist in political sentiment and a supporter of an American arms build-up during the 1950's in order to check what it viewed as the menace of Soviet and Chinese Communism. One reason why American labor, unlike labor in Italy, France, and to a lesser extent in Britain, became so strongly anti-Communist in its political orientation was the ethnic character of large segments of industrial labor. Large numbers of first- or second-generation Eastern Europeans went into the unskilled ranks of the auto and steel industries, as well as the mining industry, and they had strong memories of Soviet treatment of the Eastern European countries during and after World War II. The Irish too, who had become strong in local police and security organizations, were strongly anti-Communist in their political outlook, influenced during the early Cold War years by a strongly anti-Communist Catholic church and by certain prominent Irish political leaders, such as Senator Pat McCarran of Nevada and Senator Joseph McCarthy of Wisconsin. American labor tended to be strongly anti-Communist in political orientation, while supporting free-trade policies so long as these did not harm the labor market. In terms of influence in the setting of United States national interests, it can be said that organized labor has had greater influence during periods of Democratic presidents than Republican, largely because the Republican party owes much less to labor in return for votes delivered. Nevertheless, no administration can afford to ignore the voice of organized labor in formulating trade policies; in 1972 and 1973, for example, the Nixon administration seemed to be giving serious attention to AFL-CIO president George Meany's views on trade legislation.

ETHNIC MINORITIES

The political influence of Eastern European ethnic groups has been exerted in ways other than through labor organizations; one example is the restrictions on economic aid to Yugoslavia even though Tito broke with the Soviet Union in 1948 and followed an independent foreign policy. Secretary of State Dulles's pledge in 1953 to "roll back the Iron Curtain" was an appeal to these groups, whose political support the Republicans sought in the 1950's. When an opportunity to make good on that pledge presented itself during the Hungarian uprising in 1956, the Eisenhower administration wisely decided that the national interest of the United States did not involve risking a war with the Soviet Union over a political crisis within the Soviet sphere of influence. The result was anger among many of these ethnic minorities in the United States and disillusionment among many Eastern Europeans who took American campaign slogans more seriously than did political leaders in Washington.

Probably the most influential minority group in the United States in the post–World War II period has been the Jewish community, particularly the Zionist movement. From the early postwar period when Britain announced that it would give up its mandate in Palestine, there has been waged a powerful campaign in the United States to convince the government that the maintenance of a Jewish state in the Middle East is a vital interest of the United States. Although the Truman administration helped to create the state of Israel, the United States has not thus far made a security guarantee to Israel similar to those given to the NATO countries. Because of its concentration in New York, the Jewish population there has had a powerful influence on the politics of both political parties in that state. It has also had a large influence in the communications industry, which is largely concentrated in New York City. Campaign contributions of wealthy Jewish donors have given their views a careful hearing by leaders of both political parties and access to high government officials which no other ethnic minority has ever enjoyed in the United States. The influence of the Jewish community in this country traditionally has been greater when the Democrats have occupied the White House, although in the 1972 presidential race President Nixon gained important Jewish support and carried New York State by a comfortable margin. President Truman not only personally helped create a Jewish state in Palestine but gave it strong economic and political support in its early years. Part of this was political: the Jewish vote in New York and in other large cities was strongly Democratic; but Truman also had a deep personal conviction that the Jews who survived the Nazi concentration camps had a moral right to a homeland of their own. President Eisenhower strongly opposed Israel's invasion of Egypt in 1956 and sought to follow an "evenhanded" policy toward Israel and the Arab states. The extent of Jewish influence on Congress was demonstrated in the spring of 1970 when seventy-four senators endorsed a petition to President Nixon requesting that he sell Israel F-4 Phantom jets, which Israel had sought unsuccessfully to buy in order to continue the air war against the United Arab Republic. The large volume of news, both in the press and on television, expressing sympathy with the Israeli cause against the United Arab Republic in 1968–1970 was also an indication of the large influence of this powerful minority group in seeking to obtain United States backing for Israeli policy against the Arab States.[11]

The other major minority group, the Negroes, is slowly beginning to assert an interest in Africa as a national interest of the United States, and this emphasis is certain to grow in the future. The pressure on United States campuses for black studies programs emphasizing African history is matched by pressure from black organizations on the President to force South Africa and Rhodesia to modify repressive policies against their black populations. During the Nigerian civil war there was sentiment among some black organizations in the United States for this country to support an independent state of Biafra because many Biafrans had studied in this country and had close ties with the American Negro community. Although the influence of American Negro organizations on foreign policy is still moderate, this is likely to become stronger after the status of the American black is raised economically and he is able to devote more of his energies to foreign-policy issues.

The Mexican-American, or Spanish-American, community has not as yet asserted its voice in foreign-policy matters; however, the large number of Spanish-speaking Americans in the Southwest clearly is a political factor in elections, and both political parties have sought closer ties with Mexico in part as a means of appealing to this minority group. As with the Negro community, however, the role of Spanish-Americans in determining the national interests of this country is potential rather than real.

AGRICULTURAL ORGANIZATIONS

The political influence of farmers in the United States has diminished over the last two decades as their numbers declined, but the influence of the agricultural sector on the determination of United States interests – particularly trade interests – remains high. Few organizations have the political influence in Congress,

---

[11] This is not to say that this political effort within the United States is inconsistent with the democratic process in this country; rather, it is to underscore the great influence that this particular minority group exercises on U.S. national interests in the Middle East.

insofar as international trade policy is concerned, to match the sugar growers, dairymen, cotton farmers, cattlemen, rice producers, and wheat growers. Their political influence is far out of proportion to their numbers, but the political make-up of Congress, particularly the Southern representation, is such that rural America continues to be overrepresented in Washington. Another important factor is the effectiveness of the several national farm organizations in pressing the views of their constituents, both in the legislative and executive branches of government. Thus, in foreign-aid legislation and in negotiations under the Kennedy Round of tariff reductions among the major trading nations, the interests of American farmers and ranchers have always been forcefully represented by their organizations in contacts with the Agriculture and State departments. Although agricultural surpluses no longer are the incentive they once were in United States foreign aid programs, these farm organizations have had an important voice in determining government policy on how those surpluses were disposed of overseas. The economic benefits to American grain producers of the Soviet-American wheat sale in 1972 are a case in point, although the terms of the initial sale were questioned by some farm groups. Those associated with the foreign-affairs agencies in Washington are impressed by the continuing influence of the various farm organizations on legislation and government policy affecting imports of foreign agricultural products into the United States – even when the political interests of the country indicate that some flexibility in government policy is highly desirable. Indeed, the import quota system on certain items, and the tariff restrictions on others, have profound political repercussions in some friendly foreign countries. In Latin America, for example, if it were possible to raise the import quota or the price of commodities exported to the United States, the economic benefits to those countries might be so great as to make economic assistance unnecessary. This is not to suggest that there should be a drastic reduction of United States import controls over agricultural products from abroad, but it does mean that the power and influence of American agricultural organizations in determining

United States economic policy abroad may sometimes have an unfavorable impact on other national interests.

MILITARY-ORIENTED INDUSTRIES

Much was written about the so-called military-industrial complex during the 1960's and early 1970's, after President Eisenhower raised the question in his farewell address to the nation in 1960. Perspective on this subject is difficult to find because much of the writing tends to be sensational and raises the specter of the Pentagon, in league with certain large industries benefiting from military contracts, conspiring to keep military spending at a high level even when political trends in the world indicate that a substantial reduction of arms production might be in the national interest. The large cost overruns for major weapons systems, such as the F-111 and the C-5A, as well as for certain ship contracts and army equipment, have dramatized the high cost of military defense and given ammunition to certain congressional committees and newspapers which seek to condemn defense contractors. Some of the charges are undoubtedly true, but it is not always mentioned that defense contractors were encouraged by the Defense Department during the 1960's to speed up the time between the drawing board concept of a military item and the actual production. This was part of Secretary of Defense McNamara's effort to build up the United States' conventional military capability in the shortest possible time, so that the President would have the tools to meet non-nuclear as well as nuclear threats. Corporations whose primary client is the Department of Defense are often encouraged to take financial risks on the assumption that if their calculations prove incorrect, there will be recourse to contract renegotiation rather than the prospect of bankruptcy. No doubt some corporations and officials took advantage of the government and, in some cases, items may have been produced with enormous profit despite their marginal utility. But it is not easy to predict what kinds of military equipment might be needed to wage various kinds of wars; when Secretary McNamara set about in 1961 to provide the nation with a conventional military capability, he could not have foreseen all the contingencies under which the United States might have to engage in hostilities, and what kinds of equipment would be most suitable.

In a period of rapid military expansion, as during the Vietnam War, there will be more waste than usual in military procurement and some items may be produced that are not cost-effective; it is just as predictable that in a period of military retrenchment, scandals will be uncovered and bad judgment unearthed to show that the cost of providing national defense is too high for the nation to bear. Obviously, military contractors whose economic survival depends on defense contracts will make great efforts both in Congress and in the press to convince the public that their products are needed for national defense and that their performance in producing such equipment is at least as good as any other contractor doing business with the government. That is part of the democratic process, and the military-oriented industries have as much right to make their case to the public as the farmers, the labor organizations, and the ethnic groups. But, just as clearly, Congress has the responsibility to expose inefficiency and poor judgment in the defense industries and in the Defense Department, as in any other sector of American society. If there is too much influence on national policy-making from the makers of war materials, the responsibility is a collective one, for the amount of money a nation spends for defense and the amount of freedom it gives to military planners to determine the kinds of weapons needed is a function of the nation's assessment of the international environment. No defense manufacturer will be able to sell unneeded or vastly overpriced equipment to the government if the country is convinced that the danger of war is declining. This, in turn, is a by-product of the national consensus about what national interests are at any given time. Defense contractors have a voice in the process of creating a national mood, or consensus, about the dangers the nation faces internationally, but that voice is less effective among the public and in Congress than one would gather from reading press accounts. In the early 1970's, their fortunes declined rapidly because the mood of the country is moving away from heavy emphasis on national defense and toward domestic requirements.

VETERANS' ORGANIZATIONS AND MILITARY AUXILIARIES

If military-oriented industries exert less influence on the determination of national interests than is often assumed by the press, the influence of veterans' organizations and the civilian organizations supporting the three military services is probably greater than is generally recognized. The main reason is that, like farmer and labor organizations, they influence many votes and their voices are important in Congress. The defense-related industries may have considerable rapport with the military services, but their political influence with Congress is far less than that of the nationwide organizations which support the general concept of defense-preparedness, anti-Communism, and internal security as essential to the national interest. Although veterans groups may not have the same degree of national influence they had in the early post–World War II period and into the 1960's, their patriotic rallies and calls for strong national defense still command the attention of large numbers of middle-aged and older Americans who remember Pearl Harbor and the penalties of this nation's unpreparedness for war in 1940–1941. However, as a new generation grows up and questions the wisdom of committing large expenditures for defense, the assumptions of the veterans' organizations are being challenged. Their influence on the public clearly is declining but remains strong with many members of Congress, who represent the age group of World War II veterans.

Each of the armed services has carefully nurtured its own civilian support base as a means of bringing political pressure on Congress and the President to support the programs of the particular service. This political base has included the maintenance of strong reserve forces, the National Guard and Air National Guard, as well as such pressure groups as the Navy League, the Air Force Association, and, to a lesser extent the Association of the United States Army. The reserve components and national guard units have provided a channel for military indoctrination among younger personnel associated with the services, while the civilian associations have catered to a somewhat older group of businessmen, professional people, and others whose goals are to support a strong army, navy, or air force – and the appropriations in Congress that make this possible. There is considerable over-lapping between the leadership of these organizations and the officials of the defense-oriented industries mentioned above.

It is difficult to assess the real influence of these groups in determining national interests, but there is little doubt that they produce a large amount of publicity, sponsor radio and television programs, and inspire motion pictures that are favorable to the armed services. How much effect they have in influencing public opinion is uncertain; again, their influence is greater when the public is concerned over the safety of the nation and less when there are no foreign crises. When Stalin and Khrushchev were threatening to overrun Europe and "bury American capital-ism," it was relatively easy for the military-support groups and veterans' organizations to convince the public and Congress that large defense outlays were in the national interest. But be-ginning with the Nuclear Test Ban Treaty in 1963 and proceed-ing through the Strategic Arms Limitation Talks in the 1970's, there has arisen a new climate of opinion that challenges this view and emphasizes instead diplomacy and detente in international relations.

The international environment, then, has an important effect on the reception accorded the military-oriented organizations. The growing accommodation between the United States and the Soviet Union over arms limitation as well as a cooling of tensions in the Middle East and Southeast Asia in the 1970's may lead many more Americans to conclude that a significant reduction in defense expenditures is possible and that the government should pay greater attention to domestic needs. If an interna-tional crisis should suddenly occur – such as a Middle East confrontation – all this could change quickly, but in the ab-sense of a dramatic international crisis, the influence of the military-oriented organizations in the setting of national interests will continue to decline.

STUDENT ORGANIZATIONS

In 1965 there would have been no need to list students among groups having an influence on the national interests of the United

States. Most students were not primarily concerned with public affairs, including foreign policy, and were content to spend the major portion of their time earning degrees. The Vietnam War changed all that; not only were students directly affected by the threat of the military draft, they decided to protest also the quality of their education and the serious injustices they saw in American society. The general frustration of college youth over what many saw as a lack of any moral basis for United States involvement in the Vietnamese conflict gave radicals the opportunity they had sought for many years to politicize some campuses. The Students for a Democratic Society (SDS) and other radical student groups were more successful in some cases than others, but the publicity given to their activities by television and the press created a sense of unity among them in many parts of the country and intensified their protests against United States involvement in Vietnam. By November 1969, when some 300,000 students converged on Washington on Moratorium Day, their numbers and their strong sentiments about the Vietnam War began to be taken seriously by government leaders and many parents. Students also began to promote such causes as equality for blacks, antipollution programs, and antimilitary propaganda. Most students who participated argued that the priorities of the United States had to be changed from concentration on national security to efforts to build peace in the world; they demanded greater attention to the domestic needs of American society, even if this meant taking some risks with the security of the nation. The National Student Association, largest of the student organizations, reflected the disillusionment of college youth during its convention in Minneapolis in August 1970 and dramatized the influence of the extreme radical groups, which had lost faith in working within the constitutional system. Hearings of the Scranton Commission, which looked into campus violence in the wake of the Kent State student deaths in May 1970, also brought out the deep alienation of many students who felt ignored by government leaders. By 1972, however, the protest movement had declined significantly in intensity and influence, largely as a result of the withdrawal of half a million troops from Vietnam and the large reduction in draft calls of young men.

For our purposes here, it is sufficient to note that students will, to a degree not previously experienced in American history, try to assume the role of "watchdog" over the government in matters concerning possible military intervention abroad. President Nixon's limited engagement of United States forces in Cambodia in 1970 – which may have been a courageous military move – proved to be politically damaging among educated young people in the United States. They are likely to exert a restraining influence on the President and his cabinet members whenever a foreign problem arises that could result in sending United States forces abroad. This is not to say that students will be the decisive factor in the President's decision to use military force if he considers it in the national interest to do so; but he will have to calculate, in the foreseeable future at least, the political costs of student demonstrations if he takes actions that are strongly opposed by large numbers of students across the country.[12]

FOREIGN-AFFAIRS ORGANIZATIONS

Mention should be made of organizations whose primary mission is to inform the public about foreign affairs. The best known of these are the Council on Foreign Relations, the American Foreign Policy Association, and the Brookings Institution. All of these have staffs of experts who produce publications for the informed public on various foreign-policy problems, and they sponsor research by scholars and journalists, which is often published under their auspices. Their efforts to inform the public about the international environment and United States foreign policy gives these institutions considerable influence on the determination of national interests. *Foreign Affairs*, published quarterly by the Council on Foreign Relations, is one of the most influential journals among opinion-makers and policy-makers alike because it seeks to print the views of persons whose opinions carry considerable weight in the formulation of foreign policy. The regular meetings of the council also produce new ideas on foreign policy.

---

12 The President's careful handling of the decision to support South Vietnamese military operations in Laos early in 1971 was an indication that the lessons of the Cambodian operation of 1970 were taken into account.

The Middle East Institute, the Association for Asian Studies, and similar organizations share the objective of informing the public about events and trends in specific parts of the world. Their publications may not reach a wide audience, but they do influence opinion-makers. Foundations such as the Rockefeller Foundation, Ford Foundation, and the Carnegie Endowment also sponsor foreign-policy research that has significant influence in the determination of national interests.

THE INTELLECTUAL ELITE

In discussing the influence of private interest organizations, we were concerned with groups, not individuals; their influence is based to a large extent on significant numbers, effective organizations, and the political and economic influence they can bring to bear on Congress and the executive branch. In contrast, the term *intellectual elite* applies primarily to individual persons who, because of their intellectual, literary, or public-speaking talents, exercise significant influence over the opinions of others and, therefore, have individual impact on what Almond calls the "political and administrative elites" in government. Rosenau calls these people "opinion-makers" and defines their role as "those who occupy positions which enable them regularly to transmit, either locally or nationally, opinions about any issue to unknown persons outside of their occupational field or about more than one class of issues to unknown professional colleagues."[13] These are the persons to whom the public listens when issues in international affairs arise which are not clear to the layman, but which he feels he ought to know about in case they directly affect his life or his pocketbook. This group includes the following categories of people: syndicated columnists who comment regularly on foreign affairs; television commentators on foreign policy; university professors who write authoritatively on international affairs; researchers who write under the auspices of foundations and "think-tanks"; and certain members of the clergy whose judgment on foreign affairs is considered to be authoritative.

[13] *Public Opinion and Foreign Policy*, p. 45.

Syndicated columnists: Although it is difficult to assess the actual influence of columnists such as Walter Lippmann, David Lawrence and James Reston, their views on foreign policy and what they consider to be national interests are widely read and talked about among thoughtful Americans who are interested in the nation's role in the world. And what is more important, their views have had considerable influence on policy-makers in the government and on members of Congress who think these and other nationally read columnists are influential with the general public. During his half-century of active writing, Walter Lippmann probably had more influence on forming public opinion on many foreign policy questions (even though he was proved wrong on many occasions) than did most secretaries of state. This was because he had built up an exceptional fund of knowledge about foreign affairs (which few people outside the State Department could equal) and because he was an exceptionally effective writer. Therefore, his columns were read and talked about both in government and outside to an extent that few people other than the President himself usually enjoyed. This made Lippmann an "opinion-maker" and, indirectly, a policy-maker as well because government officials believed that he influenced a large segment of the informed public on foreign-policy issues. Although television has somewhat reduced the influence of the national columnists, officials in the State Department, Defense Department, and the White House, whose responsibility it is to assess the national interests of the United States, continue to pay close attention to the views of leading columnists who write for key newspapers circulated in Washington: the *Washington Post,* the *Washington Star,* the *New York Times,* and the *Christian Science Monitor.*[14] In addition, there are byline journalists of the major newspapers whose views on foreign affairs receive careful consideration by government officials because these journalists have developed the reputation as experts in certain areas.

Television commentators: There are fewer big names among television reporters on foreign affairs than in the press, probably

14 For a description of the influence of these "dukes" of journalism, see Stewart Alsop, *The Center* (New York, 1968), Ch. 7.

because the medium is newer and because the potential Walter Lippmanns among television personalities are not sure of the public's willingness to accept them in the role of commentator rather than reporter. The printed word, which the reader may ponder and reread, may be less threatening to his values than the television pundit whose voice must be acceptable to the ear and his facial expression pleasing to the eye before his opinions will be acceptable to the viewer's mind. The columns of the writer on foreign policy usually appeal to the reader's reason, but the television commentator often projects an emotional factor which may well distort the substance of what he is saying. Nevertheless, the television correspondents of the major networks who report regularly on foreign affairs, both from Washington and from overseas, do have influence on forming public opinion, and, as television newscasting becomes more sophisticated, it is likely that the medium will develop personalities who attract attention from wide audiences throughout the country.[15]

University professors: It would be a mistake to claim that university professors as a group command much public attention for their views on foreign policy. However, the complexity of the international environment in the past twenty years has produced a need in the public mind for expert knowledge on certain countries and on specific subjects such as nuclear strategy. Another factor giving prominence to some scholars in the academic world is the increasing number of students attending colleges and universities and their growing interest in the study of international relations. This has created a market for authoritative books on foreign countries as well as studies on United States foreign policy. Academics such as Hans Morgenthau, John Kenneth Galbraith, John Fairbank, Henry Kissinger (before joining the Nixon administration in 1969), and the many Kremlinologists have had a ready forum for their writings, which might not have made them prominent opinion-makers a generation ago. Again, the real influence of these experts is difficult to assess and the tendency probably is to overestimate their influence on the public.

[15] Walter Cronkite probably comes the closest at the beginning of the 1970's.

Another factor that gives academic specialists more notoriety than was the case previously is that television has made use of them as commentators. Thus, the television interview with an expert on China or Russia or on nuclear proliferation provides the professor with an audience for his point of view that extends far beyond the classroom. This was clearly the case during the height of the Vietnam War, when the public was concerned about large casualties, the growing opposition on campuses to the President's course, and the argument of some senators that the war was not in the national interest. In this case, the Vietnam experts had a forum far exceeding their normal university audiences, and a prominence in terms of opinion-making they never had enjoyed before and probably will not soon have again.

Experts attached to research organizations: This group of experts is similar to, but not synonymous with, the university professors. Their work is almost exclusively research, and their products are usually provided to government departments and agencies, which use them in assessing national interests and formulating foreign policies. Unlike many university professors, the individual expert working for the RAND Corporation or the Hudson Institute usually is known only to a small group of political and administrative elites. He is also known in his own profession, as most possess advanced degrees and have published scholarly articles and books, but their influence on the public at large is not great.

In terms of real influence on the determination of national interests and policy formulation, this small group of experts working in satellite research organizations has an influence on policy-makers that is far greater than persons outside the foreign affairs community of government realize. The size and influence of these research organizations grew in direct proportion to expansion of the defense and AID budgets in the postwar period, as the demand for strategic studies and foreign area studies increased. Many research specialists have been consultants to the State and Defense departments, as well as to CIA and the Agency for International Development (AID), and most of them have access to government classified information.[16] Many universities have built up institutes whose existence has depended on government research contracts. The point here is not to elaborate the extent or nature of all these research organizations doing business with the government, but rather to emphasize that individual experts in them do have an important influence on the highest policy-formulating echelons of government.[17]

Clergymen: Some writers have listed religious organizations rather than individual clergymen as having an important influence on the public's attitude about foreign affairs. They cite the pronouncements of national religious organizations on foreign affairs as reflecting the views of the millions of members these organizations claim to represent in individual church groups. However, a serious question can be raised about how much real influence a national religious organization has today on the thinking of individual church members, as exemplified by recent declines in church attendance and financial support. Clearly, the influence of the church as a social center in many American communities is far less today than it was a generation ago, and the authority of individual priests, ministers, and rabbis over the thinking of parishioners has eroded measurably. Mass communications and the high mobility of population probably account for much of the decline of church influence on individual Americans, but a change in the values of American society has also been a key factor.

Although church organizations probably are not very important in influencing public opinion on matters of foreign policy, certain well-known clergymen do have influence because of their forceful personalities, or because they have some influence on the policy-makers of the government. Billy Graham, for example, may have influence on certain foreign-policy matters because large numbers of people are attracted to his religious fundamentalism. The Reverend Theodore Hesburgh, president of the University of Notre Dame, may have some influence because he is the

---

16 Daniel Ellsberg, the RAND consultant to the Defense Department, gained notoriety in 1971 by publishing the *Pentagon Papers.*

17 Walt Rostow and Henry Kissinger, both academic specialists and consultants to the government, became presidential assistants in charge of national security affairs in the 1960's.

head of a major Catholic educational institution. Norman Vincent Peale also would have a personal following because of his intellectual abilities and moral suasion. And the Reverend Carl McIntire gained some prominence in 1970 because of his strong stand on "victory in Vietnam." But the towering preacher who commands wide attention because he understands God's Law and how national leaders should behave is a vanishing species. Individual priests and ministers may still have influence within their congregations when they apply moral standards to the conduct of foreign policy, but this marginal influence rarely extends beyond the confines of the parish. The influence of the clergy within the Catholic church may be greater than in Protestant denominations, because of the greater discipline exercised over priests by the Catholic hierarchy, but even here it is questionable how much attention individual Catholics pay to their priests' views on matters of foreign policy. The Jewish faith is another matter, because Zionism is an important part of a devout Jew's religion, and here the clergy probably exercises considerably more influence on the thinking of the layman than is the case in the Christian denominations.

The Vietnam War produced more antiwar activity among clergymen than has been the case in the United States since the 1930's. Both Protestant and Catholic clergymen participated in antiwar demonstrations and peace movements. Many ministers felt obliged to use their pulpits to question the war on moral grounds and to encourage efforts toward peace. Pope Paul also made pleas for a cessation of hostilities in Vietnam, but it is doubtful whether their appeals and activities had much influence on American public attitudes toward the war. With the strong tradition of separation of church and state in this country, there continues to be an underlying sentiment among many Americans that the church should stay out of politics. The point here is that although many clergymen feel they have a moral duty to advise their congregations – and the President – on the great matters of state, the trend in the past thirty years is for the American public to obtain its information and counsel on matters of foreign policy from other sources.

COMMUNICATIONS MEDIA

The phrase "power of the press" has long been used in the United States to describe the role of newspapers in shaping decisions on both domestic and foreign policies. However, as Stewart Alsop rightly points out in his book *The Center*,[18] power is often confused with influence. *Power* refers to the authority to make foreign-policy decisions, which is the role of the President and the Secretaries of State and Defense; the press, particularly the Washington press corps, on the other hand, has great *influence* on policy-makers in certain instances, but the press does not itself exercise power. This distinction is worth pondering because the apparent frustration of some journalists and editors probably arises from the feeling that they should have greater influence than they do – even to the point of helping to exercise power in the sense of making decisions. George Reedy goes so far as to say that many newspaper stories, and a much higher number of columns, are written "solely for their impact upon the President," and he observes that "newspapermen are not exempt from the universal urge to shape history." [19]

When we talk about the influence of the press and other communications media in the shaping of national interests on any given foreign issue, we can look at the question in terms of the impact the media have on the general public – the way in which reporting of the news causes the public to react positively or negatively to whatever it is that the President wants to do. Obviously, this is important to any discussion of the role of the communications media in the formulation of national interests, as was shown by the nature of the television coverage of the Vietnam War. But the media, and particularly the press, have a more direct impact on the shaping of national interests because the Washington press corps, which Alsop estimates to number about fifteen hundred, is in constant contact with the key policy-makers, and it is in a position to ask embarrassing questions which government leaders might otherwise not be forced to address. James

[18] P. 155.
[19] *The Twilight of the Presidency* (New York, 1970), p. 100.

Reston, in his book *The Artillery of the Press*, recalls that after the Bay of Pigs debacle in 1961, President Kennedy told the managing editor of the *New York Times* that he wished the press had disclosed much more of the secret information it had about the planned invasion of Cuba because the reaction of the public might have caused him to cancel the operation.[20] George Reedy, who is concerned about presidential blunders in foreign policy because of the President's growing isolation from the people, observes that the press is one of the few social institutions that "keep a President in touch with reality." "It is the only force," he says, "to enter the White House from the outside world with a direct impact upon the man in the Oval Room which cannot be softened by intermediary interpreters or deflected by sympathetic attendants."[21] Reedy believes that the real influence of the press upon the President lies in its capacity to tell him how he is doing, as seen through other eyes, a service which rarely will be performed by any other medium. Yet Reedy admits that even among the White House press corps there is a reluctance to be really frank with a chief executive about his actions, because the President can cut off their source of information – and thereby their effectiveness as White House reporters – simply by ignoring them.

Granted, then, that the press does exercise significant influence in the determination of national interests, what are the limits of its responsibilities? Here Reedy parts company with some of his newspaper colleagues, saying that "a reporter has no business selecting his stories on the basis of the national interest" because he is doing the national interest a disservice. "The closest he can come to it and still remain true to his trade is to report what others conceive to be 'in the national interest.' This is a point which no successful politician can grasp."[22] In other words, a good newspaperman should not try to play the role of policymaker.

Another aspect of the question is: What are the responsibilities of the press, television in particular, to refrain from divulging

[20] (New York, 1966), p. 31.
[21] *The Twilight of the Presidency*, p. 99.
[22] Ibid., p. 114.

information that might bring harm to the national interest? The issue was brought into sharp focus in 1971 when Daniel Ellsberg leaked the secret Pentagon Papers to the *New York Times*, which decided to publish them. Here there are few guidelines, because the First Amendment to the Constitution has given the press greater latitude than in most Western countries to determine for itself what the public has a right to know – even when this conflicts with government policy. The restraints are political rather than legal in this country, and a newspaper that consistently steps over what are considered by the government to be the bounds of security is likely to be cut off from whatever sources of information it did enjoy.[23]

Apart from the influence the Washington press corps has on policy-makers, they and their colleagues have a key role in keeping the public informed of what is going on in the State Department, the Pentagon, and, where possible, the National Security Council. If the public is to perform any real function in the formulation of national interests, these opinion elites, as they are sometimes called, need a steady flow of accurate news upon which to make their judgments. James Reston believes that the media need to do a better job on this score. "The problem is to present the great issues as a series of practical choices; let the people look at the alternatives as the President has to look at them and try at the end to decide among the hard and dangerous courses."[24] This view assumes that the public not only has a right to know what the options are, but that our democratic system makes it imperative that the public has a say in the choices; this is so that the President does not make decisions that will be rejected by the people when the true costs of the choices become known.[25]

Television has become the most important medium for informing the general public of what is going on in the world, and much has been written about the effects of television on the public's attitude toward the Vietnam conflict. But the news mag-

[23] For a scholarly discussion of the role of the press in policy formulation, see Bernard Cohen, *The Press and Foreign Policy* (Princeton, N.J., 1963).

[24] *Artillery of the Press*, p. 87.

[25] In my view, this was a principal failure of President Johnson's handling of the Vietnam escalation from 1966 to 1968.

azines and influential daily newspapers, with their interpretive reporting, probably have a greater impact on the attitudes of opinion elites, because they are influenced in their thinking more by the printed word than by the visual image of the news. Although motion pictures have declined in importance as a medium since the advent of television, the impact of certain types of motion pictures on intelligent young people should not be underestimated. The movie "Z," for example, had an important impact on college youth, as did the films "Fail-Safe" and "Dr. Strangelove." These political films may not be patronized by the mass public, but they attract large numbers of college youth and shape their views on foreign and defense policy.

Although government leaders deplore the divisive effects on public opinion of television coverage of controversial events, there is also the view that television might become the captive of the President. Reedy believes that television in the hands of a skillful President could be a danger to our form of government. The presidential news conference, he says, is so carefully staged that any President who handles himself moderately well will dominate not only the whole proceeding but also the news shows that report the conference. "What has really happened is that a device universally hailed as a boon to communication has become a one-way street. It is a means by which a man can conduct a monologue in public and convince himself that he is conducting a dialogue with the public."[26] This is a serious charge, and it should give pause to those who argue that television networks must be restrained by government in the type of coverage they employ on national news shows. If the President is always in a position to dominate the airwaves with his view of a foreign crisis and his view of the national interest, would it not be dangerous if legal restrictions were imposed on the way in which television networks report news that is in conflict with the President's view? If, as Reedy argues persuasively, the President is increasingly isolated from the political realities in which the public views the world, is it wise in a democratic society such as ours to further isolate him from these realities (against which his judgments are

[26] *The Twilight of the Presidency*, p. 165.

made about national interests) by restricting both his and the public's exposure to opposing viewpoints? This question is as difficult to answer as the question of the proper relationship between the President and Congress in foreign-policy making, and in the use of the armed forces. The question finally comes down to how much one is willing to trust the judgment of one man in matters of war and peace.

PRIVATE INTEREST GROUPS, MASS MEDIA, AND NATIONAL INTERESTS

Although there is always the danger of oversimplifying any categorization of interest groups, there is an advantage to thinking about the objectives of these groups in terms of their impact on certain kinds of national interests. If we conclude that the basic national interests of the United States are the product of the aspirations and demands of the American people – reflected and defined by their elected representatives – then a more precise description of how the objectives of these various private groups fit into the total national interest of the country is advantageous. Using the three categories of basic national interests set forth in Chapter 1, we may then list private interest groups and members of the intellectual community as representing primarily the following points of view:

NATIONAL DEFENSE

Veterans' organizations
Military auxiliaries
Defense-oriented industries
Ethnic minority organizations
Defense-oriented research organizations

TRADE AND COMMERCE

Business groups
Financial organizations
Labor
Agriculture

WORLD PEACE AND ORDER

Students
Professors
Clergymen
Intellectuals

This list does not include two of the most influential groups mentioned earlier in this discussion, syndicated columnists and television commentators. This is because they do not fit primarily into any one of the three categories but span all of them. The same is true of the communications media and public affairs groups. But, granted that newspapers, news magazines, and television networks do represent all three basic national interests to one degree or another, it is a matter of some concern to government leaders that the emphasis is not always evenly spread. For example, the Nixon administration became frustrated during its first two years in office over what it believed to be the antagonism of the "liberal Eastern press" and of a number of television commentators to its foreign policies. Vice-President Spiro Agnew became the administration's spokesman in singling out these antagonistic newspapers and commentators, in part accusing them of playing with the nation's security by failing to support the President's policies in Southeast Asia as well as his major defense programs, such as the antiballistic missile system for protection of the country's nuclear deterrent. In effect, the Vice President accused certain news media and national news commentators of not being concerned with the national defense interests of the United States.

The frustration of government leaders with the media, regardless of the party in power, arises from the fact that the Eastern press and the major television news shows have a disproportionate influence on the administrative elite, as Almond calls it, and also on intellectual groups that exercise a large influence on students throughout the country. If the *New York Times* and *Washington Post* agreed with the administration's view of the nation's interests, there would be little reason for the President to be disturbed about their influence. It is because they disagree on some fundamental points with the President's perception of America's role in the world and because they have considerable influence in molding the views of the administrative elite that their role is so irritating. Presidents Truman, Eisenhower, Kennedy, Johnson, and Nixon have all shown anger over the criticism that the Eastern press and certain television commentators have voiced over their handling of foreign affairs. In the 1972 presidential election campaign, Senator George McGovern also showed irritation with the press for allegedly distorting his views on both his domestic and foreign policy proposals. Even some liberal writers lamented the vagueness of his proposals – and their modification during the campaign.

In the final analysis, the President must be able to appeal successfully to the electorate over the heads of his opposition in the press and television, as well as his opposition in Congress, if he wishes to have his view of the national interest validated. The press and television have a responsibility to question the president's actions even when the criticism seems unfair or misguided. As Reedy points out, a President can always command the front pages of the nation's newspapers and prime time on television when he speaks to the nation. The problem is not his opportunity to be heard, but rather whether his view of national interests is realistic enough to be supported by a majority of the people, over a sufficiently long period, to make it possible for him to formulate and carry out a consistent foreign policy. From 1945 until roughly 1960, there was national consensus that defense was America's most important interest. By 1970, this assumption was clearly in doubt, and the President could ignore this change only at high political risk.

5

Foreign Policy Tools in Support of National Interests

OUR DISCUSSION has centered so far on the development of a conceptual framework for defining national interests more accurately, and on assessing the influence that the President, Congress, and private-interest groups exert in the process of determining the degree of interest, or the stake, the United States has in various international issues. Now we turn to the instruments or tools of policy that the President has at his disposal to support national interests, and here we come to the key question of how policy tools may be made the handmaiden of national interests rather than determinants of interests, as has often been the case since World War II. Another way of stating this issue is: Are assessments of interests made on the basis of the values and costs outlined in Chapter 2, or are they determined by the availability of powerful policy tools at any given time?

Before dealing with this crucial question, it is well to enumerate the various foreign-policy instruments at the President's disposal to deal with threats to United States interests abroad, starting with those entailing modest influence on an adversary and moving to those carrying the greatest amount of pressure or power. The discussion is divided into the four levels of interest described in Chapter 1: peripheral, major, vital, and survival.

PERIPHERAL INTERESTS

Diplomacy: Diplomatic communication between governments is the normal means by which sovereign states seek to resolve conflicting interests without resort to war. Diplomatic negotiations support the entire range of United States interests, from peripheral to survival, and nations find ways to communicate even when they do not have formal diplomatic relations. The United Nations serves as a forum where informal discussions between states can take place outside normal diplomatic channels. For example, the Korean War was brought to a conclusion through informal contacts initiated at the United Nations between United States and Soviet representatives. Also, Peking and Washington have carried on talks for years, even though no diplomatic relations existed between them. This situation changed early in 1973, however, when Washington and Peking agreed to establish "liaison offices" and appoint high-ranking diplomats to each other's capital.

Diplomatic exchanges are usually handled between the embassies maintained in various capitals and may be transmitted through the foreign ambassador in the home country or through one's own ambassador in the foreign country. In handling problems that involve only peripheral interests, that is, those that affect private citizens or firms having business in a foreign country, the normal channel is the commercial or the consular section of an American embassy abroad or of a consulate general. If an American merchant vessel has difficulties in a foreign port, it is the consular officer of the American embassy who seeks, through a local government ministry, to obtain a solution to the problem. An American businessman who receives unfair treatment in a foreign country usually will bring his case to the commercial section of the embassy and seek help through diplomatic means. Although this aspect of diplomatic activity abroad is largely ignored by the press and television because it is so routine, these efforts to protect the interests of American firms and American citizens abroad consume a large proportion of the work load of any United States diplomatic mission. This function is primarily the responsibility of the Department of State, which acts as agent for many other departments and agencies of government doing business overseas, including Commerce, Treasury, Agriculture, Labor, Justice, Transportation, and a number of independent agencies whose operations involve them in dealings with foreign governments. In fact, most government departments and agencies have created separate international divisions whose function is to work with the State Department to find solutions to problems that have international implications. From time to time both the State Department and other departments have been frustrated, feeling that the State Department is not adequately equipped to handle the extra burden that the business of other agencies abroad represents. In fact, only about one-fifth of United States personnel serving in American diplomatic missions abroad in 1972 were State Department personnel.[1]

Educational, cultural, and scientific exchanges: Ever since the end of World War II the United States has placed great emphasis on increasing communications between the peoples of other countries and the American people. An important part of this effort is the exchange of students, professors, scholars, scientists, political leaders, artists, writers, and musicians. Early in the postwar period, Congress enacted legislation establishing the Fulbright Program, which provided an opportunity for many foreign students and scholars to study in the United States and for American students and scholars to study and do research abroad. Another important piece of legislation in this field, the Smith-Mundt Act, made it possible for leaders and specialists of foreign countries to visit the United States and learn about American institutions and culture. American professionals similarly were able to go abroad to exchange ideas and knowledge with foreign counterparts. These programs were subsequently expanded under State Department auspices to include performing arts groups. Beginning in the Eisenhower administration, this People-to-People Program rested on the assumption that if citizens of other countries had greater contact with Americans of similar interests, better relations between the countries would be promoted. Implicit in this activity is the idea that American interests and policies will be enhanced if there exists a friendly psychological climate within other countries.

[1] This factor has been debated for years within the State Department and has resulted in several reorganizations to make the Foreign Service more responsive to the needs of other agencies as well as the desires of the political leadership in the White House. The latest effort was launched in 1970 under the theme *Diplomacy for the 1970's: A Program of Management Reform for the Department of State* (Washington, D.C., 1970).

Educational, cultural, and scientific exchanges are listed as tools in support of peripheral interests not because they are peripheral activities but because their intended effect – building understanding between peoples of different nations – is a long-range, relatively nonpolitical mission and because curtailment of the activity does not pose a serious danger to American interests abroad. For example, when United States–Soviet relations were strained following the Soviet armed intervention in Czechoslovakia in 1968, cultural exchanges were suspended by the United States to show its displeasure; however, the suspension itself did not seriously affect relations between the two nations and exchanges were resumed early in the 1970's.

Humanitarian assistance: Another important and relatively nonpolitical program at the President's disposal is humanitarian assistance, which includes disaster relief, support for refugees, and food-assistance programs. Normally, these are short-term efforts to aid the victims of floods, famines, earthquakes, and wars. Much of this aid is channeled through international relief organizations, but a substantial amount is also provided directly by the United States. This assistance, which is controlled by the State Department, has been extended to nearly every part of the world in the post–World War II period without regard to the political ideologies of the countries suffering from calamity. Many agencies of the United States government are involved in administering this program, including the armed services, which have the capability to move quickly anywhere in the world when disaster strikes.

Technical assistance: Providing expert knowledge to underdeveloped countries to assist in their economic development was started by President Truman in his Point 4 program in an effort to influence the policies of new nations in Asia and Africa. Like cultural and scientific exchanges, this program emphasizes human resources rather than financial assistance. Under this program, administered by the Agency for International Development (AID) and its predecessor agencies, American specialists in such fields as agriculture, transportation, and medical sciences are sent to foreign countries to assist in improving the local standard of living. Most Peace Corps volunteers who work abroad also fit into this category. Much of this technical assistance is administered by American universities, which recruit the specialists who work abroad. Foreign trainees in many fields of endeavor also are brought to the United States to gain knowledge in these fields and apply it at home. Some material assistance is available under this program, but it is in direct support of specific projects where foreign peoples are learning to help themselves.

Technical assistance, like cultural and scientific exchange programs, is essentially nonpolitical in nature and is designed to promote goodwill toward the United States and its people. It does not involve large outlays of funds, compared with economic and military assistance, nor does it involve the prestige of the United States to any significant degree if such aid is withdrawn. Nevertheless such aid is a source of influence with many less developed countries which need such help in building their economies.

Propaganda: Beginning in World War II, the United States embarked on a foreign information program, which continued after the war and today is an important tool in the conduct of American foreign policy. The official propaganda,[2] or information effort, of the United States government consists of many activities, including official statements of the President and the Secretaries of State and Defense, background briefings by high officials in the administration, Voice of America programs beamed to the Soviet Union and other Communist-dominated countries, United States Information Service libraries located throughout the world, and television shows and motion pictures shown abroad with the consent of the host countries. The United States Information Agency (USIA) has responsibility for disseminating information overseas about United States policies and of presenting a balanced picture of American life and institutions to foreign audiences. It has no responsibilities within the United States.

---

[2] The term *propaganda* is used here in its traditional meaning, namely, to propagate or inform – not in the sense of the Nazi German period when the word came into disrepute.

One of the challenges, and sometimes problems, which a free society such as the United States has in carrying on a foreign information program is that the picture it gives of the United States may be at variance with the view of America disseminated abroad by the American press and television and the news media of foreign countries, which have ready access to the same facts as does the official information agency. And if the picture received by foreign peoples from their own media differs substantially from what they get on Voice of America and from other official American sources, they are likely to disregard the views expressed by the American government. This is particularly true in the case of United States government policy. The job of USIA is to see that a full and accurate picture of these policies is disseminated abroad and it must, therefore, establish a credibility among foreign audiences for unbiased reporting. Otherwise, its message will not be believed and its effect would be only marginal.

The question must then be addressed: How important a policy tool is propaganda in furthering the national interests of the United States? The answer is that, like diplomatic intercourse and cultural exchanges, it is a low-risk activity in most foreign countries and contributes to a better understanding and appreciation of American policies and intentions. However, it is problematical whether the short-run objectives of an information program conducted by the United States are of great significance in furthering the national interest; it is more likely that the longer-range cultural programs conducted by USIA and the State Department overseas have a more lasting impact on foreign people and on their attitudes toward the United States and American institutions. There are few instances in which the United States has been able to influence a foreign government to change its policy primarily through use of propaganda tools.

MAJOR INTERESTS

Economic assistance: Financial assistance to support a nation's economy and economic aid to promote its development are tools of policy that carry with them the assumption that the recipient country is sufficiently important to the national interest of the United States that its economic well-being and political institutions should be supported by a considerable outlay of American economic resources. Most of the countries that have received large amounts of United States economic aid have been allied with this country in mutual security arrangements, either bilateral or multilateral.[3] But a security pact is not a precondition for such assistance in some instances; for example, the United States provided substantial economic assistance to India and to Indonesia in the 1950's, even though both countries refused to join in the Southeast Asia Treaty with the United States and chose instead to follow a nonaligned foreign policy. Conclusion of an economic assistance agreement with a foreign government entails obligations both on the part of the United States and the recipient nation, and such agreements make clear that mutual political interests form the underpinning of the agreement. It is patently incorrect to view economic assistance agreements between the United States and foreign countries as having no political strings attached, for if there were no political objectives that the United States and the recipient could agree upon, it is unlikely that Congress would be willing to vote the large sums involved in their implementation. If the programs were for economic purposes only, it might be more profitable for both countries to have such aid channeled through international agencies, especially the United Nations.[4] This is not to say that the United States has not, and will not in the future, give economic assistance unless its security interests are at stake; in some cases – Indonesia being an example – the United States may have an important economic reason for providing aid – to develop markets for its exports and investment opportunities for American private capital. The security question may be involved, but at a different level. The point here is that the American government, and most other governments, do not provide large-scale economic assistance abroad without considering political objectives. Most other major lending nations such as Japan, Britain, France, and Germany are

---

[3] Thailand, Turkey, Korea, Taiwan, and Iran have been major recipients.

[4] Even in this case the U.S. would have a political objective in building stability within the country and perhaps providing markets for U.S. products.

much more forthright than the United States in admitting that they have political objectives in assisting underdeveloped countries. Perhaps this is a reason why the American people and Congress have become disenchanted over economic assistance programs since the mid-1960's – they have not been convinced by the executive branch, AID in particular, that there is a clear political objective to be served in providing substantial assistance to certain countries.

Economic and trade policy: One way the United States shows concern in a foreign-policy issue and exerts pressure on another nation is by regulating its trade with that country. The United States maintains import quotas on many foreign products, for example, sugar, coffee, oil, meat, and dairy products. Certain countries that depend on the United States market can be vitally affected by a change in the import quota or by other acts that restrict their ability to sell in the United States. Hence, the threat of such action by the United States is a means of exerting pressure on another nation. The United States can also bring political influence to bear by refusing to extend credits and financial assistance to a requesting country, and by discouraging the flow of private American capital to that country. Because of its heavy financial support for various international lending organizations, the United States can also exert considerable influence on the decisions of these organizations to aid or not to aid individual nations needing support. And finally, as the United States dollar is the primary international currency, its stability is a key factor in the economic life of many nations, both developed and underdeveloped. When the United States decides to devalue the dollar, as it did in 1971 and 1973, this action sends shock waves over the world and causes major trading nations many economic and political problems.[5]

Trade policy as a tool of national policy is more effective against smaller nations and underdeveloped countries than against large and powerful ones because the United States itself

[5] It should be noted, however, that U.S. actions in 1971 to restrict imports and force an upward revaluation of other currencies was a drastic action and probably signaled that vital, not just major, economic interests were at stake.

is subject to retaliation from large trading nations such as Britain, Japan, and Germany. Until 1972, trade policy had little effect on societies such as the Soviet Union, Communist China, or Poland because their economic well-being did not depend on trade with the United States. In 1970 the case of Japanese textiles became an issue when United States textile producers brought pressure on Congress to pass restrictive legislation on textile imports because they threatened serious harm to domestic industries. Negotiations with the Japanese government eventually produced a voluntary agreement by Japan to limit the amount of textile exports to the United States, but the case highlighted the importance of trade policy as a means of bringing pressure on another nation when one's major economic interests are involved. It also points up the fact that, unlike defense interests, economic and trade policy may be used as a weapon against friendly and even allied countries. This is a relatively new development in postwar United States foreign policy because only recently has it become necessary for the United States to take actions to warn its allies against what American policy-makers consider unfair trade policies.

The principal United States agency involved in formulating and executing trade policy is the State Department, but other departments and agencies also have a large voice in determining these policies. Treasury and Commerce as well as Agriculture and the Tariff Commission are involved in setting international economic policy; in the Nixon administration a new coordination staff was set up in the White House, the Council on International Economic Policy, to insure that the efforts of various agencies are consonant with the President's views. The Interior Department also plays a key role in this field because it administers the oil import quotas, an important political issue in many parts of the United States and in oil-producing countries abroad.

Clandestine operations: The United States as well as all great powers carry on intelligence activities in other countries, but normally they do not wish to be associated officially with these activities. Influencing the decisions of key foreign officials is a primary objective of clandestine operations, as is gathering of intelligence about the intentions of foreign governments. These activities may include the training and equipping of foreign forces to fight against certain governments unfriendly to the United States, or to support other governments that do not wish to enter into a formal military alliance with the United States or accept its military assistance. The Central Intelligence Agency is the primary arm of the government in the clandestine field, and its personnel are located in many countries. However, the Defense Department also carries on extensive clandestine activities, particularly in the collection of information about military activities and intentions of potentially hostile nations. The difference between these operations and other tools of policy that the United States government employs to further its national interests is that a primary objective of clandestine operations is to influence the actions of individuals and groups within a foreign country. The methods employed often are those with which the United States government does not wish to be associated, but which it finds necessary to support in order to achieve its objectives in a world where most nations use any means at their disposal to achieve their national objectives. Although some Americans are opposed to using what they consider to be unethical means to gather information or to influence the behavior of foreign officials, it is nevertheless true that this country and most others would not be able to protect their interests to the same extent, and might even endanger their security, if they refused to engage in clandestine activities.

In a world where a nation can be destroyed in a few hours, accurate intelligence of an enemy's intentions is an absolute necessity for a great power such as the United States. To refuse to engage in clandestine activities because it hurts the sensibilities of certain groups would be as foolhardy as refusing to take a vaccination because it puts germs into the human system. Had it not been for the U-2 flights of the 1950's, for example, the United States would not have got an accurate picture of Soviet missile capabilities. Similarly, spy ships such as the *Pueblo* served an indispensable need in helping to assess the intentions of potentially hostile nations. Of course, the failure of a covert operation, such as the Bay of Pigs episode in 1961, causes the public to question whether such activities should be conducted at all, because the price of failure and exposure of involvement make the value of the operation questionable. In 1961 President Kennedy corrected what he perceived to be serious defects in the scope of certain types of clandestine operations and in the coordination of these activities with government agencies that must bear responsibility for such actions in case of failure. Today clandestine activities are under the careful scrutiny of the highest levels of government, and fewer mistakes are made. But such operations are, without question, an important tool in the conduct of international relations, and there is no major interest of the United States in which the gathering of information is not important to the protection of those interests.[6]

Military assistance: A decision to grant military assistance to a foreign government is a clear signal that at least a major national interest is involved in protecting that country against foreign pressure or subversion. Providing military assistance also bolsters the foreign regime's ability to handle its own internal security problems and, unlike economic and technical assistance, tends to strengthen the hand of the government in dealing with its opposition. This is particularly true when the recipient government is controlled by military forces or is strongly supported by them.

Military assistance was designed originally to bolster the defenses of allied countries against Communist pressure and possible attack. However, military assistance was extended also to certain nonallied countries – Indonesia and Cambodia, for example – because it was thought to be advantageous to American interests to establish good relations with military officers in such countries. Training of foreign military officers in the United States has been an important means of assistance, as it brought these men into contact with Americans and, it was hoped, gave them a better appreciation of the United States and its policies than they might have received in their own countries. Also, military aid has been given in some cases to prevent the acceptance of aid from the Soviet Union and other Communist countries.

[6] One of the most perceptive insights into CIA operations may be found in Stewart Alsop, *The Center* (New York, 1968), Ch. 8.

Military assistance, like economic aid, has always had political strings, and such aid gives the United States an important influence on internal conditions in the recipient country. However, this program has spawned large United States military assistance groups (MAAGS) in many countries, and the size of these staffs has had a considerable impact on the American presence in many countries, particularly those located near the Soviet and Chinese borders.[7]

A real problem with military assistance programs is that they tend to involve the United States in the internal affairs of foreign nations to such an extent that there is a considerable tendency for its interests to escalate in proportion to the amount of aid given. In other words, except in countries where there is a clear threat of overt attack, there is a propensity for the interest to grow from a major to a vital one because there is a large United States military presence. When American advisers help a foreign government to deal with insurgents as part of an internal security program, there tends to be created a national interest in supporting that foreign government even when it deals with its legitimate, non-Communist opposition. During the 1950's and early 1960's, when United States policy was based on anti-Communism, it was easy to equate political opposition in some underdeveloped countries with Communist subversion; therefore, aid to a government to stamp it out was considered to be in the national interest. Today, however, this view of the world is no longer defensible, and military assistance likewise is being called into question where it tends to perpetuate unpopular foreign regimes in power – particularly unpopular military regimes.

Thus, military assistance in the future may have to be considered a tool of policy to support only vital, not major, United States interests – to be given only to countries in danger of external attack and whose security is considered vital to American interests. This would reduce the number of countries receiving military aid and would greatly reduce the size of the United States military presence in many countries. At the present time,

---

[7] Many of the larger military assistance missions were substantially reduced during the first Nixon administration, along with reductions in other U.S. overseas activities.

however, the use of military assistance must still be viewed as a tool also supporting major interests because such programs continue in many countries where vital interests clearly are not at stake.[8]

Military show of force: If the President is sufficiently concerned about a danger to the nation's defense, to its economic well-being, or to world order, he may decide to make a military show of force to impress on a potentially hostile power the seriousness with which the United States views the situation. A show of force is designed to demonstrate not only that a nation has the military power to challenge objectionable moves by an adversary but also that the nation's leadership has the will to employ the power, if necessary, to protect its interests.[9] For a land power, such as the Soviet Union, the primary means of making a show of force is to mass an army or hold military maneuvers near the area being contested. For the United States and other maritime powers, the navy has been the traditional means of bringing military pressure to bear on an adversary. Later, air power was also employed with some effectiveness. For example, during the 1950's the Strategic Air Command was a primary means by which the United States signaled to the Soviet Union and other countries its concern over international issues. Deployments of the Sixth Fleet in the Mediterranean and the Seventh Fleet in the western Pacific today are the principal means by which the United States shows its concern over security threats in the Middle East and in Southeast Asia. The President may also appeal to the American public regarding a foreign crisis, as a means of warning an enemy nation of his concern.

   Although a show of military force is employed primarily when

----

[8] In 1971–1972, there was great competition between the State Department and the Defense Department over which would get control over the proposed new Security Assistance Program, recommended by the Peterson Commission to replace military and police assistance in the Foreign Assistance Act. The State Department won this battle.

[9] A show of force was an important means of signaling the intentions of great powers during the nineteenth and early twentieth centuries, when balance-of-power politics was the basis for international behavior. With the rise of superpowers in the post–World War II era, this means of communication of intentions has been restricted largely to them.

threats to a nation's defense interests are involved, it may also be used to support economic and world-order interests. British and French use of forces in Egypt in 1956 was probably motivated more by concern for Middle East oil than for either nation's defense needs in the eastern Mediterranean, from which both had largely withdrawn after World War II. World order (balance of power) interests accounted for United States concern over the fate of Jordan in 1970 and of Pakistan in 1971.

The danger in embarking on a show of force, as a tool of policy, is that it must be credible to both the adversary and to other countries, or it runs the serious risk of being taken for a bluff. A show of force that is made with no real intention of backing it up with additional force if the adversary does not cease his action can produce a highly dangerous situation because national prestige becomes a key factor. When Secretary of State Dulles talked of a policy of "brinkmanship," he was referring to the threat of nuclear retaliation against the Soviet Union if it did not refrain from actions strongly opposed by Washington. This show-of-force policy was realistic only so long as the United States had a clear strategic superiority over the U.S.S.R. When nuclear parity was reached in the 1960's, this policy was no longer credible either to the Soviets or to America's allies because a refusal of a great power to compromise could be catastrophic in the nuclear age. This is because neither side can be sure that the adversary will not use nuclear weapons rather than suffer a disastrous defeat.

Thus, we may conclude that the show-of-force tool of national policy lies on the borderline between a major and a vital interest. It is clear that Presidents have used this policy tool to defend major interests in the past, such as in the Taiwan Strait crisis of 1958 and the Lebanon crisis in the same year. But the question remains whether additional force would have been employed if the show of force had failed. Here is where it is essential that the President be clear in his own mind just how much value should be attached to a particular issue. If he makes a show of force and it is seen as a bluff by the other side, he must be prepared either (1) to back down and admit that the issue was not in fact vital, or (2) to escalate the involvement and pay the price of going into limited war. Neither alternative is attractive to a chief executive, particularly when there is no strong public support for the perceived interest.[10]

Economic sanctions and naval blockade: Sanctions may be imposed against a country that threatens the vital interests of another or threatens the political and economic stability in a given area. These include a trade embargo, impounding of assets, interference in trade with third countries, and the like. The United States employed these policies against Germany and Japan during World War II and, to a limited extent, against the Soviet Union and Eastern European countries during the 1950's when the Cold War was at its height. History shows, however, that economic sanctions do not usually work unless they are supported by military force – particularly by a blockade. The League of Nations' economic sanctions against Italy in 1935 after its aggression in Ethiopia did not succeed, and British sanctions against Rhodesia in the 1960's similarly were unsuccessful. Ten years of trade embargo by the United States against Cuba also did not result in the ousting of Fidel Castro, or in changing his policies toward the United States. This is because sanctions require either (1) agreement among all major trading nations not to deal with a given country, or (2) the willingness of at least one great power to impose a blockade, which constitutes an act of war. Thus, the United States, for all its naval and air power, has refrained from employing the risky tactic of a blockade, except in the case of the Cuban Missile Crisis in 1962, when it used the measure but called it a "quarantine" to differentiate it from a total trade blockade.

Economic sanctions against a hostile nation may be employed when a vital interest is at stake, and occasionally when an important major economic interest is threatened; but military measures, such as a naval blockade of an enemy's ports and interference with its shipping, normally would not be employed unless the United States also contemplates armed intervention. This

10 This is nowhere better illustrated than in the reluctant decision of several presidents to escalate U.S. involvement in Vietnam (see Ch. 6).

was demonstrated in President Johnson's refusal to order a blockade of Haiphong Harbor during the Vietnam War. Although a blockade probably would have gravely affected North Vietnam's ability to continue the war, the risks of provoking a larger war with the Soviet Union implicit in such a policy were considered to be too high in view of his limited war objectives in Vietnam. In effect, President Johnson decided that Vietnam was not so vital that he would risk war with China and the Soviet Union. By 1972, however, President Nixon had improved United States relations with both powers to the extent that he felt safe in ordering the mining of Haiphong Harbor after North Vietnam launched an offensive in the South in April of that year.

The navy traditionally is the agent for carrying out a blockade, and the State and Commerce departments have responsibility for imposing economic sanctions. However, when the President decides to impose a naval blockade, all the armed services would probably be put on alert status because the consequences of such actions may involve military conflict.

Armed intervention: The principal additional means that the President may employ when he determines that the nation's vital interests are at stake is the deployment of ground and air forces in combat operations. Such action is taken only after all other policy measures cited above have failed to deter an enemy from a course of action that threatens the vital interests of the United States. Unlike a show of force, where the navy and air force are the primary tools of policy, the army is usually the primary agent for implementing a policy of protecting vital national interests. This was true in Korea in 1950, in Vietnam in 1965, and also in the Dominican Republic in 1965. It has also been true in Germany, although in the case of the Berlin Blockade in 1948–1949, the air force was the means by which President Truman showed that a vital American interest was involved. One may make a case that the landing of troops in Lebanon in 1958 was an indication of a vital United States interest in the Middle East; however, President Eisenhower correctly calculated that these troops, mostly marines, would not have to fight unless the Soviets intervened. Thus, it appeared to be a show of force.

The problem with a policy of military intervention to support a vital interest is the difficulty in containing such a conflict for two reasons: (1) the enemy may obtain increasing support from a powerful ally and thus force an escalation of the conflict, and (2) political pressures at home for a military victory may force the President to go beyond what he would otherwise think was prudent in terms of the limited military objectives. When armed intervention is undertaken, the military build-up often instigates a momentum of its own and each step of intervention tends to build a rationale for additional escalation. Thus, war aims become a critical factor whenever limited military force is used in support of vital interests. Unless the President clearly perceives the limits of his own objectives and is able to communicate them to the electorate, he runs a considerable risk of being forced by events to get involved far more deeply than the nation's total national interests would warrant. Clearly, President Truman found himself in this situation in Korea in 1950; so did President Kennedy at the height of the Bay of Pigs adventure in 1961; and President Johnson was forced by military as well as political circumstances to become more deeply involved in Vietnam in 1966 and 1967 than he had originally anticipated.[11]

It is important to note that on this priority scale of national interests, the defense of a vital interest does not include the use of massive military force but only the limited use of force. All-out military force would be used only in cases of national survival, that is, the threat of invasion or of nuclear attack. It is here that some confusion has arisen among the American people over war aims because, some observers argued, if South Korea and South Vietnam were so important to the United States that it sent large military forces to defend them, the President should not have refrained from bombing Chinese territory and invading North Vietnam to force a settlement. The answer is that both wars were intended as limited military engagements for limited objectives, and this clearly did not put either conflict in the category of a survival interest. The President runs considerable political risks

11 Some may argue that President Nixon faced a similar dilemma in the spring of 1970 when he decided to send U.S. forces into Cambodia for two months, even though he had announced that the U.S. was withdrawing its forces from Vietnam.

when the limited use of force fails to achieve the desired objective, for he must then decide whether the national interest is worth the additional force that might be used, and the additional risks of a wider war. That is why a prudent president must carefully weigh the costs and benefits of an armed intervention, especially if the duration of the conflict is not predictable with any degree of certainty.

SURVIVAL INTERESTS

We have defined survival interests as those that involve an immediate danger to the security of one's homeland – not of allies – and thus may require all-out effort by the nation to prevent a nuclear attack and, if that proves impossible, to survive a nuclear confrontation. In a period when there is nuclear parity between the superpowers, a surprise attack is less likely so long as rational men are in control of governments. But assuming that a nuclear exchange could conceivably result from a breakdown of communications or from an irrational action, it is reasonable to assume that top priority must be given to diplomatic negotiations in order to reduce misunderstandings and create a climate in which accommodation of national interests of the superpowers can take place. This is clearly the purpose of the SALT negotiations, which commenced in Helsinki in 1969 and led to the Moscow Accords of May 1972. In addition to these diplomatic efforts, however, the President will take other steps to prepare the country for an emergency situation when he perceives that a threat to the survival interests of the nation may be at hand.

Mobilization: In time of national emergency the President has broad powers to employ all the resources of the nation to withstand a military attack. Many such measures were employed during World Wars I and II when the nation's human and material resources were diverted for the war effort. A partial mobilization took place during the Korean War, but not during the Vietnam conflict.

Many constitutional rights may be abrogated during a national emergency, as was the case during the Civil War and to some extent in both world wars. The fear of a Japanese attack on the West Coast of the United States in 1941–1942 caused the authorities to uproot thousands of American citizens of Japanese origin and place them in quarantine in the interior of the country. Restraints on freedom of speech as well as censorship of mail and news are normal measures taken during time of war to protect the security of the nation. In the event of a nuclear threat to the nation, dispersal of population from large cities would be instituted, and major functions of government would be relocated in safe areas. Military forces would assume a large role in maintaining public order and safety, and there would be severe limitations on travel. The government would take over control of transportation and communications. In fact, if the survival of the nation were clearly at stake, parts of the country could take on the character of a garrison state. This is because a nation that values its institutions and way of life will usually do whatever is necessary in order to survive, rather than submit to a hostile power if it believes it has a reasonable chance of survival. This was the position Britain found itself in in 1940 when it seemed inevitable that Hitler would successfully conquer the nation after he crushed the rest of Western Europe in a matter of a few months. It is unlikely that the United States would submit to nuclear blackmail by the Soviet Union or any other nuclear power so long as it had the capability for resistance. The experience of the Cuban Missile Crisis seemed to confirm this instinct of the American people.

When the President is convinced that a threat to the survival interests of the nation is present, he will declare a national emergency and assume war powers, either with or without a specific declaration of war by Congress. In the nuclear age, time may not permit the exercise of the Congress's constitutional right to declare war and the President may communicate with a few members of Congress about what needs to be done. When he declares a national emergency, all agencies of government will be mobilized to deal with the emergency, but the primary ones will be the Defense Department and the Office of Emergency Preparedness (OEP). Although the latter does not receive public attention during peacetime, the Director of OEP is a statutory member of the National Security Council and would assume great authority over the civilian life of the nation in case of a national emergency.

Nuclear alert: If there is a clear threat of attack on the United States, the President has power to alert the nuclear retaliatory forces of the nation and, if necessary, to institute a nuclear attack on enemy installations. When a vital interest approaching a survival interest is at stake, the President may put the nuclear forces on alert in order to warn the enemy that he is prepared to use them if the latter does not stop pursuing a particular course of action. If neither the nuclear alert nor the initiation of a limited conventional attack deters the enemy from using nuclear weapons against the United States, the President would use all the forces at his disposal to limit the damage to the United States. This is one reason why both President Johnson and President Nixon placed considerable emphasis on the deployment of an ABM system in the United States – to limit the amount of damage that could be done to United States retaliatory forces and to American cities if all other efforts failed to prevent nuclear war.

The purpose here is not to describe in detail what actions the President would or should take if a situation developed in which survival interests appeared to be threatened. Rather, it is to emphasize that this is clearly a matter where the nation itself would be threatened with disaster – not just an ally or even some American armed forces. The threat to use nuclear weapons would be the last resort to convince an enemy that a survival interest was at stake. Chairman Khrushchev probably did not believe in June 1961 that President Kennedy meant it when he said the United States would risk a war to save Berlin. Fortunately, the Soviet leader did not push his campaign of harassment in Berlin to the breaking point, but miscalculations of this kind could conceivably result in nuclear conflict, and the President lives at all times with the knowledge that he has the power wherever he moves to unleash nuclear war if the survival interests of the nation demand it. Even if one argues that the actual use of nuclear weapons negates the question of security for countless American citizens, one cannot avoid the argument that a failure to have such weapons, and the willingness to use them in self-

FIGURE 1

National Interests and Tools of Policy: Defense

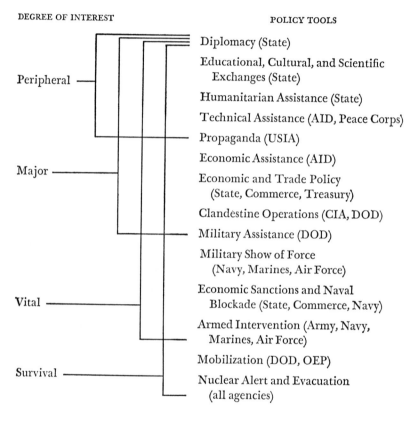

DEGREE OF INTEREST

POLICY TOOLS

Peripheral

Major

Vital

Survival

Diplomacy (State)

Educational, Cultural, and Scientific Exchanges (State)

Humanitarian Assistance (State)

Technical Assistance (AID, Peace Corps)

Propaganda (USIA)

Economic Assistance (AID)

Economic and Trade Policy (State, Commerce, Treasury)

Clandestine Operations (CIA, DOD)

Military Assistance (DOD)

Military Show of Force (Navy, Marines, Air Force)

Economic Sanctions and Naval Blockade (State, Commerce, Navy)

Armed Intervention (Army, Navy, Marines, Air Force)

Mobilization (DOD, OEP)

Nuclear Alert and Evacuation (all agencies)

defense, would be a sure invitation to an enemy to use conventional military power to pressure its adversaries.

NATIONAL INTERESTS AND SELECTION OF POLICY TOOLS

From this enumeration and discussion of the various instruments of policy available to the President to deal with threats to United States interests, it should be apparent that there ought to be some correlation between the amount of pressure to be exerted and the degree of interest involved in any specific foreign-policy issue. Figures 1–3 illustrate this proposition more clearly.

FIGURE 2

National Interests and Tools of Policy: Economic

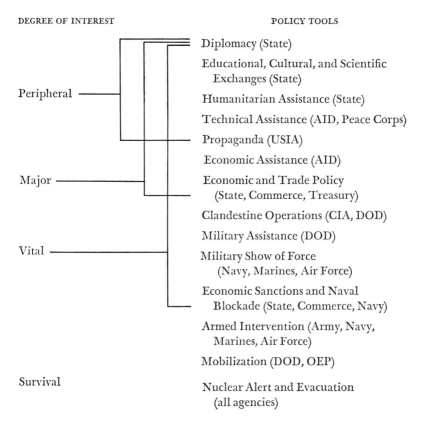

DEGREE OF INTEREST

POLICY TOOLS

Peripheral

Major

Vital

Survival

Diplomacy (State)

Educational, Cultural, and Scientific
Exchanges (State)

Humanitarian Assistance (State)

Technical Assistance (AID, Peace Corps)

Propaganda (USIA)

Economic Assistance (AID)

Economic and Trade Policy
(State, Commerce, Treasury)

Clandestine Operations (CIA, DOD)

Military Assistance (DOD)

Military Show of Force
(Navy, Marines, Air Force)

Economic Sanctions and Naval
Blockade (State, Commerce, Navy)

Armed Intervention (Army, Navy,
Marines, Air Force)

Mobilization (DOD, OEP)

Nuclear Alert and Evacuation
(all agencies)

What is suggested here is that for each of the three basic national interests outlined in Chapter 1 – defense, economic, world peace and order – there is a difference in the degree of interest involved and the appropriate policy tools to be employed to defend it. For example, if the basic interest is national defense – protection of United States territory – there is no question at all that the armed forces would be used if the degree of interest is perceived by the President and Congress to be vital. This was clearly the case during the Cuban Missile Crisis when the threat was to the United States itself; President Kennedy was prepared to invade

FIGURE 3

National Interests and Tools of Policy: World Order

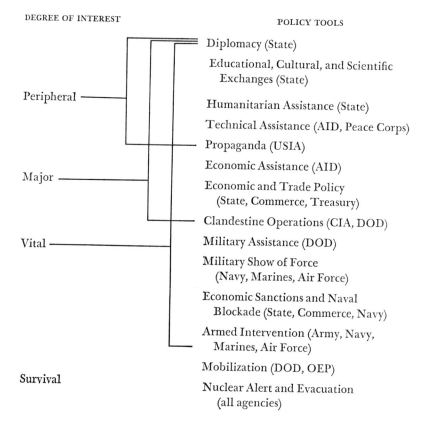

DEGREE OF INTEREST

POLICY TOOLS

Peripheral

Major

Vital

Survival

Diplomacy (State)

Educational, Cultural, and Scientific Exchanges (State)

Humanitarian Assistance (State)

Technical Assistance (AID, Peace Corps)

Propaganda (USIA)

Economic Assistance (AID)

Economic and Trade Policy (State, Commerce, Treasury)

Clandestine Operations (CIA, DOD)

Military Assistance (DOD)

Military Show of Force (Navy, Marines, Air Force)

Economic Sanctions and Naval Blockade (State, Commerce, Navy)

Armed Intervention (Army, Navy, Marines, Air Force)

Mobilization (DOD, OEP)

Nuclear Alert and Evacuation (all agencies)

Cuba if necessary to prevent the establishment of Soviet missile sites there. Similarly, a perceived survival interest would clearly entail a willingness to use nuclear weapons if that were finally the only means of warning an attacker that the United States would not capitulate in the face of an ultimatum.

On the other hand, if the basic interest is economic, even when the degree of interest is perceived as vital, the President probably would not contemplate using armed forces but would take strong economic measures, including economic sanctions. Most issues involving economic interests fall into the major or peripheral category and are usually dealt with by diplomatic means. However, when the health of the entire United States economy is endangered by pressure from abroad, as President Nixon clearly decided in August 1971, the President will take stronger measures to alter the situation, including economic retaliation against foreign currencies, trade restrictions, and perhaps an embargo on trade.

In the event of a threat to world peace and order, if the situation affects the vital interests of the United States – for example, an armed attack on a country whose defense is considered vital to United States security – the President might then use limited forces to warn the attacker, but he would try to prevent the expansion of the war and seek a negotiated settlement at the least cost to the United States. Thus, an important conclusion to be drawn from this elaboration of interests and policy tools is that only in the case of threat to the territory of the United States itself would a survival interest be at stake and justify the use of nuclear weapons. Neither in the case of economic interests nor of world order interests should the President contemplate nuclear weapons. The only possible exception in which nuclear weapons might be used when United States territory is not threatened is in the case of a key ally to which the United States has given a nuclear protection guarantee. Japan and Canada are examples.

We come, then, to the central point of this discussion: Has the United States since 1945 permitted its international interests – world peace and order – to become globalist because of the availability of vast economic and military power to support an American hegemony? In restrospect, the answer probably has to be answered in the affirmative. The fact of American atomic and nuclear superiority in the twenty years after World War II probably caused the nation's political leadership to go farther than it might otherwise have gone in relying on military power not only to achieve national defense goals but also to further economic and world order interests as well. This might have been perceived as wise policy so long as it did not entail too high risks for the defense of the United States, nor cost too much in terms of American lives and economic resources. By 1965, however, the basis on which this globalist policy was built was disintegrating: nuclear superiority over the Soviet Union had given way to nuclear parity, and the cost of supporting American world-order interests was being questioned by an increasing number of Americans. The Vietnam War proved to be the tipping point in the United States' willingness to bear the burden of protecting the world order established after World War II, just as World War I was the high point in British willingness to maintain the Pax Britannia established in the nineteenth century.

Now that a nuclear balance has been achieved by the Soviet Union, the question must be asked: Can the United States realistically contemplate the use of conventional military power anywhere in the world in the future as a tool of national policy? Another way of stating this is: Are United States interests in many parts of the world vital, or are they only major? And, if they are not vital, is it necessary or desirable that United States military forces should be based in those areas, particularly when their presence may tend to create a vital interest? If American military and economic strength is to be employed in an area that is not directly related to the defense of the United States, is it not better that this be done in concert with other great powers, or under international sanction, rather than because American prestige is involved as a result of the presence of American forces in the area?

These are difficult questions to answer categorically because world-order interests are more ambiguous than either defense or economic interests. Yet, the Vietnam experience has shown that American interests in Southeast Asia had far less to do with the intrinsic value of the area to United States interests than balance-of-power considerations. The history of United States involvement in Vietnam also shows that the nation's prestige was more involved because of the presence of its military advisers there after 1954 than might have been the case if the Eisenhower and Kennedy administrations had clearly stated that the nation's vital interests were not at stake after the French withdrew in 1954.[12] Berlin could have been a similar situation, although here the value of the territory was perceived to be high by four American presidents, and European allies presumably would have

12 See Ch. 6.

supported a United States stand there, whereas they did not in Southeast Asia. Nevertheless, the presence of United States forces in Berlin was a key factor in United States policy – in effect, they were hostages to insure that if the Soviets or East Germany moved forces into West Berlin, they would be engaged by United States troops, not only European troops. The agreements reached in 1972 between the two Germanys and between the Soviet Union and the three Western powers greatly reduced the possibility that war would result from a confrontation in Berlin.

Ideally, there should be some method by which the President can decide both the level of United States interest and the policy tools to be used to protect that interest on the basis of mathematical calculations. Although this is unlikely ever to become a reality because politicians and statesmen will continue to rely on their best judgment rather than scientific formulas to decide national interests and foreign policy, it may nevertheless be of some value to attach numerical ratings to interests and tie policy tools to those numerical ratings in a fashion that more clearly identifies the limits of policies to be used in any given foreign issue. For example, if a scale of 1 to 10 were used to measure the degree of each value described in Chapter 2 when assessing the importance of a foreign threat to American interests, the highest score would be 70, which clearly would mean a survival interest was involved. Similarly if the total score for the seven value factors came out to 40, one might conclude that a high major interest was at stake. The same kind of scoring might be attached to costs, with possible nuclear war representing 60 at the top of the scale and no risks having 0 points at the bottom. If the value score were high and cost score were low, the President's decision would be easy, but if both value and cost scores were high, for example, 55 on value and 50 on cost, then the problem would be complex; and the job of policy-makers would be to judge the amount of risk involved in using specific policy tools. The instruments of policy could also be given scores, from 1 on cultural exchanges to 100 for a nuclear strike against an enemy; the judgment would have to be whether armed intervention in a third country would be justified in light of the scores obtained on the values and costs.

The purpose here is not to devise mathematical formulas for

decision-making on national interests and foreign-policy actions, but to suggest that decisions on use of tools must be more closely tied to the degree of interest involved. The United States can no longer afford the miscalculation of its interests that occurred in Vietnam, nor of the policies employed there to defend those interests.

6

Changing Perceptions of United States Interests in Southeast Asia: A Case Study

NO PROBLEM in the post–World War II period has vexed American presidents and policy-makers more than the seemingly simple question: How important to our national interests is the area in Southeast Asia known as Indochina? Prior to World War II the United States had practically no interests in this region because it was part of the French colonial empire and cut off from trade and commerce with this country. The Philippines constituted the farthest westward security interest of the United States in the Pacific, and even this interest dated only from the turn of the century when President McKinley decided to annex the territory from Spain. Nevertheless, in the span of only twenty years, Southeast Asia and Indochina came to be perceived by American leaders as a vital national interest, one so important to United States interests in Asia that it would eventually require half a million troops to defend and a cost in excess of 50,000 American lives.

How was it possible that in two decades the United States' perception of its national interests in this exotic and backward area of Asia, so remote from America in history, culture, and politics, could escalate from the peripheral to the vital interest category? In the simplest terms, Indochina represents the best example in postwar United States policy of how the nation misjudged its vital interests and, as a result, gradually took on what many critics now call an imperial role in the world. What started out in the early postwar period as an acknowledgment that the United States had vital interests at stake in preserving a friendly and economically viable Europe gradually came to be transformed into a global view that America's interests were intimately tied up with helping non-Communist nations when they were threatened with external or internal Communist pressure. The Truman Doctrine of the late 1940's soon was expanded into an American responsibility to accept the task of containing Communism everywhere, on the assumption that peace is indivisible and that no other nation had the power and the willingness to assume the role of world policeman.

Indochina was not unique in America's perception of its worldwide responsibilities for maintaining peace and freedom; what made this area – Vietnam specifically – different was that the cost of upholding the perception of a vital interest there proved to be far in excess of what any policy-maker had foreseen, and eventually the government was forced to alter its view of the degree of national interest involved there. That change in perception is nowhere more clearly stated than in the Nixon Doctrine, enunciated by the President in Guam in the summer of 1969 and elaborated in subsequent statements of United States foreign policy. Vietnam probably is the high-water mark of the postwar imperial outlook of the United States; it is, therefore, of some interest to look back over thirty years to see how the American view of its interests in Indochina has changed, and the reasons for these changes. In doing so, we will make use of the conceptual framework for determining national interests outlined in Chapters 1 and 2, and of the policy tools described in Chapter 5.

ROOSEVELT'S PERCEPTION OF UNITED STATES INTERESTS

The Roosevelt administration realized in 1940 the possibility that Japan might turn its attention to Southeast Asia rather than continue to concentrate its expansionist effort in Northeast Asia. This prospect increased in the summer of 1940 when Japan demanded and received from Vichy France, which continued to administer French colonial possessions in the Far East, permission to use the Tonkin area of North Vietnam as an invasion route to South China. From that time, it might be said that United States concern over Japanese intentions in Southeast Asia moved to the major interest level. The State Department began giving Indochina considerable attention – not because of great attachment for the area itself, but because of the likelihood that Japan would use Vietnam as a jumping-off point for a much more ambitious effort to take over all of Southeast Asia with its large resources and strategic waterways between the Pacific and Indian oceans. To show its concern over Japanese intentions, the United States government imposed a partial trade embargo on Japan in the summer of 1940 and indicated through diplomatic channels the seriousness with which it viewed Japanese movements southward in Asia. Several members of Roosevelt's cabinet, notably Secretary of War Henry Stimson and Secretary of the Treasury Henry Morgenthau, urged the President to confront Japan in 1940 over its war against China, as well as the move into North Vietnam; but others, particularly Secretary of State Cordell Hull, cautioned the President against any action that might result in war because they believed the country was not prepared for a war in the Pacific. The American Ambassador to Tokyo, Joseph Grew, counseled the President to attempt a compromise settlement with moderate elements in the Japanese government, headed by Prince Konoye, because he did not believe that war between the United States and Japan was in either nation's interest. President Roosevelt appeared to vacillate between the conflicting views of America's interest in the growing conflict with Japan, much to the despair of Secretary Stimson.[1]

In July 1941 the Roosevelt administration apparently came to the conclusion that Japan's ambitions in Southeast Asia were real and that the United States had a vital interest in preventing Japan from gaining control of the resources of that area. Japan precipitated this change of policy by moving troops into South Vietnam in late July and declaring a protectorate over all of French Indochina. This bold action by Japan, only one month after Hitler's armies attacked the Soviet Union in Europe, convinced Secretary Hull that the time had come for action; shortly

[1] See James MacGregor Burns, *Roosevelt, the Soldier of Freedom, 1940–45* (New York, 1970), Ch. 4, for a detailed account of the discussions that went on within the administration over policy toward Japan in 1940–1941.

thereafter, the United States froze all Japanese assets in the United States and embargoed oil shipments to Japan. This was a serious action for the United States to take, for it was clear to anyone who knew about Japan's heavy dependence on United States oil to fuel its war industries that Japan either would have to give up its ambitious plan to extend the East Asia Co-Prosperity Sphere or make an all-out effort to take over the Dutch East Indies with its large oil resources. The latter course clearly carried the risk of war with the United States.[2] The two governments negotiated for five months in the hope of reaching some understanding that would prevent war; however, even though the Konoye government in the fall of 1941 appeared willing to make concessions on the issue of South Vietnam, it was unwilling to give up its war in China. Thus, war between the two nations became inevitable, and the only question remaining in late November 1941 was: where would Japan strike?

In the fall of 1941, therefore, the United States government had clearly come to the conclusion that stopping the Japanese advance into Southeast Asia – in effect, Japan's domination of all East Asia – was a vital interest of the United States and must be opposed with the force of arms.[3] It is of some historical importance that the Roosevelt administration's decision to confront Japan in the Far East was precipitated by Japan's move into South Vietnam in July 1941. This move was so clearly a threat to the balance of power in Asia that Roosevelt was finally convinced that the United States probably could not avoid war with Japan. In 1941, therefore, it was Vietnam that set the United States on a collision course with Japan; yet, Indochina itself was not a vital interest of the United States, only the issue (like Czechoslovakia in 1939) that finally convinced a great power that it could no longer negotiate over matters that threatened to upset the power balance and eventually affect its own safety.

Having made his stand on Indochina in 1941, President Roosevelt throughout the war was determined that France should not

[2] The process by which the U.S. government imposed the embargo on oil is described in Dean Acheson, *Present at the Creation* (New York, 1969), pp. 24–26.

[3] The breakdown of these negotiations with Japan in the fall of 1941 is discussed in Norman A. Graebner, Gilbert C. Fite, and Philip L. White, *A History of the United States* (New York, 1970), 2:734–35.

be permitted to return there after the war and reestablish its colonial control. He believed that a trusteeship should be established under United Nations auspices and that the peoples of Indo-china should be given independence as soon as they were capable of receiving it. He had instructed General Albert Wedemeyer in China not to give any supplies to French forces in Indochina, and he refused to provide ships to French forces that were to be sent there when the war was over. On his way home from the Yalta Conference early in 1945, Roosevelt told reporters that he had been worried about Indochina for two years and had asked Chinese leader Chiang Kai-shek at the Cairo Conference whether China wanted a piece of the area. Chiang declined but was opposed to the French going back. Soviet Premier Stalin liked the trusteeship idea, Roosevelt said, but British Prime Minister Churchill was opposed because it "might bust up their empire."[4] Roosevelt's biographer, James MacGregor Burns, believed that although Roosevelt was serious about the trusteeship idea he was not willing to break up the Atlantic Alliance over it. Both the British and French were opposed, and their cooperation in Europe in the postwar period would be essential if Europe was to be rebuilt. "The President had anti-colonial ideas; what he lacked was a carefully conceived strategy to carry them out, given the global strategic considerations and the checkered and volatile politics of Southeast Asia."[5]

TRUMAN'S PERCEPTION OF UNITED STATES INTERESTS

Roosevelt died before the lines were clearly drawn on United States policy in Southeast Asia in the postwar period. President Truman did not have the strong anticolonialist idealism of Roosevelt, and he approached the question in more pragmatic fashion. The view of the State Department in 1945 was that Europe was paramount insofar as United States worldwide interests were concerned, and although there was little disposition to help the French to reestablish their colonial empire in Southeast Asia, there also was no disposition to antagonize the French

[4] Burns, *Roosevelt*, p. 592.
[5] Ibid., p. 593.

by actively subverting their interests there. Therefore, in the fall of 1945, the United States did not oppose the French return to Indochina; neither did it provide France any help to do so, and it continued to voice its preference for self-government for the colonial peoples. Indeed, the United States gave no encouragement to the Viet-Minh leader in 1945, Ho Chi-Minh, who made several overtures to American officials in Hanoi seeking United States government recognition for an independent state of Vietnam.[6]

It might be concluded that in 1945, the American interest in Indochina had declined to a peripheral one, wherein the United States would take no active part in shaping the destiny of that part of Asia, leaving it to the French to provide whatever leadership and security were needed. In effect, the United States government considered Indochina to be rather low on its list of international priorities, clearly far below its preoccupation with rebuilding Europe. It was a period of "benign neglect."

The year 1950 marked a significant shift in the United States' perception of its interests in the Far East generally, and in Southeast Asia specifically. This resulted in large measure from the victory of the Chinese Communists on the mainland in 1949 and the subsequent visit of Mao Tse-tung to Moscow, where he concluded a defense treaty with the Soviet Union in February 1950. In view of Stalin's bold efforts in Europe in 1948–1949 to prevent formation of the North Atlantic Pact and Peking's strong anti-American statements and actions after the Red Army took control of the mainland, Washington came to the conclusion that it would henceforth have to deal with a Sino-Soviet Bloc whose ambition was to drive the United States out of Asia as well as Europe and establish its own hegemony. Soviet acquisition of its first atomic weapon late in 1949 added to the sense of urgency in the Truman administration to develop new policies to deal with the Soviet and Chinese threat in the Far East.[7]

It had already become apparent in 1949 to United States

---

[6] Ho's appeal is reported in one of the documents contained in the *Pentagon Papers*, published by Bantam Books (1971), p. 25, entitled "Report of Ho's Appeals to U.S. in '46 to Support Independence."

[7] The reassessment of U.S. worldwide policies early in 1950 is described in Acheson, *Present at the Creation*, Ch. 41.

policy-makers that if the French position in Indochina had any long-term hope of success, France would have to grant independence to the Associated States of Vietnam, Laos, and Cambodia. Vietnam was the key, and by the end of 1949 France concluded an agreement with Prince Bao Dai giving him control over internal affairs in the Republic of Vietnam, which then became independent within the French Union. Once the republic was legally established, the United States and other non-Communist nations granted diplomatic recognition to the Bao Dai government. Predictably the Soviet Union and China granted recognition to Ho Chi-Minh's government as the legal authority for all Vietnam, and the lines for the struggle in Vietnam were thus sharply drawn already in February 1950. President Truman moved in May 1950 to provide economic and military assistance to the French in Indochina, as Paris was opposed to any direct dealings between the United States and the new Republic of Vietnam. As Dean Acheson recalls in his memoirs, there were great misgivings within the State Department over whether such aid to Indochina would in fact lead to the defeat of the Communist insurgency there; the State Department doubted that the French would ever train the Vietnamese to fight their own war and let the Bao Dai government exercise real internal authority in the new nation. Acheson describes the dilemma of Indochina in the spring of 1950 as follows: "The criticism, however, fails to recognize the limits on the extent to which one may successfully coerce an ally. Withholding help and exhorting the ally or its opponent can be effective only when the ally can do nothing without help. . . . Furthermore, the result of withholding help to France would, at most, have removed the colonial power. It could not have made the resulting situation a beneficial one either for Indochina or for Southeast Asia, or in the more important effort of furthering the stability and defense of Europe."[8]

Acheson thus confirmed what critics of American policy in Vietnam have said for many years: United States policy was guided more by its perception of interests in Europe than by a realistic appraisal of France's ability to defeat a Communist insurgency in Southeast Asia. The important point, for our pur-

[8] Ibid., p. 671.

poses, is that in the spring of 1950, President Truman changed his perception of United States interests in Indochina and implicitly acknowledged that the degree of interest had risen from peripheral to major. The granting of economic and military assistance was confirmation of this changed view. But as in 1941, the interest had as much, or more, to do with factors outside Vietnam than with the struggle within this Asian territory; the United States needed a strong French ally in Europe and in the Far East and so it supported France's basic interests there, rather than staking out an independent assessment of its own interests.

The outbreak of war in Korea confirmed, not created, the new perception of United States interest in Indochina. Suddenly, it became clear that the Soviet Union would resort to war to gain its objectives if it thought it had a reasonably good chance of accomplishing them without a large risk to itself. China's entry into that war seemed to confirm the monolith concept of international Communism, and the policies of the United States moved from diplomacy and aid to emphasis on military strength and alliance systems. In this situation concerns about whether aid to France in Indochina would be effective in dealing with the insurgency became almost academic. With national attention focused on the war in Korea, the United States needed a strong French ally more than ever, both for participation in the United Nations effort in Korea and in the new defense structure of the North Atlantic Alliance. The degree of United States interest in Indochina and in other parts of Southeast Asia remained major, however, because there was no intention of using American forces; but the importance of helping France to defeat the insurgency in Indochina rose considerably after the outbreak of hostilities in Korea, and within a few months United States military and economic aid for the French effort increased substantially. Predictably, the French proved to be adamant in refusing to permit the United States to interfere with their policies in Indochina. Acheson recalls that General de Lattre de Tassigny, French commander in the area, paid several visits to Washington, demanding more and faster aid and "to urge us to declare that loss of Indochina would be a catastrophic blow to the free world; yet he resented inquiries about his military plans and his intentions regarding transfer of authority to the three states [Vietnam, Laos, Cambodia]."[9] The former Secretary of State also recalled that in the autumn of 1951 the Joint Chiefs of Staff warned the administration against making any statements that "would commit – or seem to the French under future eventualities to commit – United States armed forces to Indochina. We did not waver from this policy."[10] In other words, the United States government was not prepared to say that the vital interests of France in Southeast Asia were also the vital interests of the United States. President Truman was willing to give France very large assistance to keep her involved as an ally in the Far East, but he was not willing to use American forces for that purpose. Therefore, during the Truman administration, Indochina moved from a peripheral to major interest and remained there.

EISENHOWER'S PERCEPTION OF INTERESTS

By 1954 the French people were weary of the war and the French government was looking for ways to negotiate an end to the struggle that would permit France to maintain a presence in Indochina. The Eisenhower administration, however, looked upon a negotiated settlement as tantamount to a crushing political defeat for the Western position in Asia and sought to bolster French confidence. But the French plan for winning the war – the Navarre Plan – was not successful, and a sizable French force was faced with disaster near the Laotian border at Dien Bien Phu. To President Eisenhower, who had advised the French against the Dien Bien Phu operation, the reality had to be faced that France would give up the struggle in Vietnam and that the Viet-Minh would then extend Communist control over the whole of Indochina and threaten Thailand.

In the early months of 1954, the United States had to reassess its national interests in Indochina and decide whether its loss to hostile forces was a vital matter for the United States, or whether it could live with a negotiated settlement of the war. Eisenhower wrote: "As I viewed the prospects of military intervention in the

9 Ibid., p. 675.
10 Ibid.

relative calm of early 1954, it seemed clear that if three basic requirements were fulfilled, the United States could properly and effectively render real help in winning the war. The first requirement was a legal right under international law; second, was a favorable climate of Free World opinion; and third, favorable action by the Congress."[11] He did not find that the first requirement presented a difficult problem because France, and presumably the Bao Dai government, would have requested such intervention. But on conditions two and three there were difficulties. The key to the second, Free World support, was the attitude of the British government, and the Churchill cabinet at that time showed great reluctance to join a Free World coalition to save the French position in Indochina. The British were inclined to see whether negotiations at Geneva to end the Korean War might produce some compromise settlement also in Indochina; Churchill, therefore, let Eisenhower and Secretary of State Dulles know that he wished first to explore the diplomatic route before contemplating military moves. As for congressional approval, it became clear that Senate leaders would not approve of a unilateral United States military action to save the French position. Congressional support would be conditional: (1) other free nations including the British Commonwealth must participate in the undertaking; (2) France had to give greater independence to the Associated States, so there would be no appearance of aid to French colonialism; and (3) France must remain in the struggle. President Eisenhower agreed with these points and instructed Dulles to make them known to other nations concerned with the problem of Indochina.

Throughout the critical months of early 1954, the key question for President Eisenhower was whether to commit United States ground troops to Indochina. Vice President Nixon had suggested in a talk before the American Society of Newspaper Editors on April 16 that the President might have to take that step in order to prevent further Communist expansion in Asia. But the President could not bring himself to do so even though he knew that a failure to act probably would result in a French

[11] See Dwight D. Eisenhower, *Mandate for Change* (Garden City, N.Y., 1963), p. 340.

withdrawal from the war. To quote Eisenhower: "The ever-present, persistent, gnawing possibility was that of employing our ground forces in Indochina. . . . I let it be known that I would never agree to send our ground forces as mere reinforcements for French units, to be used only as they saw fit. Part of my fundamental concept of the Presidency is that we have a constitutional government and only when there is a sudden, unforeseen emergency should the President put us into war without congressional action." [12] Secretary of State Dulles cautioned against committing United States prestige in Indochina when he told French military leaders in Paris in March 1954 that "if the United States sent its flag and its own military establishment – land, sea or air – into the Indo-China war, then the prestige of the United States would be engaged to a point where we would want to have a success. We could not afford thus to engage the prestige of the United States and suffer a defeat which would have worldwide repercussions." [13]

The pressures on the President in April to consider bombing strikes to relieve the French garrison at Dien Bien Phu were great, especially from the Chairman of the Joint Chiefs of Staff, Admiral Radford, who shared the French view that the fall of Dien Bien Phu would cause France to abandon Indochina. However, the President was adamant that the United States should not intervene without allies because he could not obtain congressional approval to act alone. The French garrison fell on May 7 and France thereafter negotiated a settlement that partitioned Vietnam at the seventeenth parallel between the Viet Minh and non-Communist forces.

The lesson of 1954, insofar as the perception of United States interests in Indochina was concerned, is that the President and his advisers wrestled with the question whether Vietnam was vital and, in the final analysis, decided it was not – at least not in the circumstances that prevailed at that time. Therefore, despite the large investment in arms and economic aid to the French, the United States decided that its stake in Indochina was not so great that it should use its own forces to prevent a French

12 Ibid., p. 345.
13 Ibid.

defeat. Whether the outcome would have been different had the French agreed to give the United States an independent role in fighting the Communist insurgents will never be known, but the evidence seems to suggest that President Eisenhower was not willing to send any forces to Indochina unless the British were willing to join that effort. Thus, in deciding whether Indochina was a vital American interest, the President gave great weight to one of the seven value factors described in Chapter 2 – attitude of key allies. If the President had had strong support in Congress for intervention, he might not have needed British support; however, with only lukewarm support in Congress, he needed British cooperation for domestic political reasons.

Another President, ten years later, when faced with similar problems in deciding whether to intervene in Vietnam, came to a different conclusion. But the situation had changed in those ten years and with it the perceptions of intelligent men. That is why it is essential to look at the situation, both foreign and domestic, faced by each President when judging his perception of the national interest. Eisenhower in 1954 apparently was willing to face the consequences of a French withdrawal from Southeast Asia and the southward expansion of Communist power. In hindsight, it may be said that United States prestige did not suffer seriously from this decision, nor did the President's political fortunes at home. However, the decision not to intervene in 1954 did not solve the problem of Vietnam, or of southeast Asia. It only meant that the problem was put off for awhile, for another President to grapple with.

REASSESSMENT OF INTERESTS BY THE KENNEDY ADMINISTRATION

By 1961, the Geneva Accords of 1954, which partitioned Vietnam and confirmed the independence of Laos and Cambodia, had come unstuck. The Laotian political crisis of 1960 produced a security crisis in the spring of 1961, and the new Kennedy administration decided to negotiate a *de facto* partition of Laos and a coalition government in Vientiane rather than use force to prop up the rightist regime of General Phoumi Nosavan. Thereafter, the focus of attention turned to South Vietnam where the Viet Cong had begun an insurgency campaign against the government of Ngo Dinh Diem, while North Vietnam was sending large supplies down the Ho Chi Minh Trail to support them. From the spring of 1961, therefore, the Kennedy administration was seized with the problem of what to do about South Vietnam: was it worth trying to save, and what was it likely to cost? In effect, it was the same question President Eisenhower wrestled with seven years earlier, in different circumstances: Was Vietnam vital to United States interests in the Far East?

The *Pentagon Papers* published by the *New York Times* and several other American newspapers in June and July 1971 have shed new light on the decisions that were made by the Kennedy administration in 1961 regarding the degree of United States interest involved in Vietnam and the policies adopted to support that interest. It is desirable, therefore, to probe this record to find the basis for American military intervention four years later.

The record now shows that President Kennedy made his decisions on Vietnam following strong recommendations from his Vice President, Lyndon Johnson, who had visited Vietnam and Thailand in May, and after a survey, in October, of the security situation in Vietnam by two key presidential advisers, General Maxwell Taylor and Walt Rostow. Vice President Johnson summed up his findings as follows: "The fundamental decision required of the United States – and time is of the greatest importance – is whether we are to attempt to meet the challenge of Communist expansion now in Southeast Asia by a major effort in support of the forces of freedom in the area or throw in the towel." The Vice President was not suggesting that this was a simple choice, for he went on to point out the possible costs involved: "This decision must be made in a full realization of the very heavy and continuing costs involved in terms of money, of effort and of United States prestige. It must be made with the knowledge that at some point we may be faced with the further decision of whether we commit major United States forces to the area or cut our losses and withdraw should our other efforts fail." Finally, Johnson called attention to the wider aspects of this crucial decision for United States policy: "What we do in Southeast Asia should be part of a rational program to meet the threat we face in the region as a whole. It should include a clear-cut pattern of specific contributions to be expected by each partner according to his ability and resources. I recommend we proceed with a clear-cut and strong program of action." [14]

General Taylor put the question of American interests in a wider context, namely, dealing effectively with Communist unconventional warfare: "Communist strategy aims to gain control of Southeast Asia by methods of subversion and guerrilla war which by-pass conventional U. S. and indigenous strength on the ground. The interim Communist goal – en route to total takeover – appears to be a neutral Southeast Asia, detached from U. S. protection. This strategy is well on the way to success in Vietnam." Taylor referred to "a double crisis of confidence" in Vietnam and Southeast Asia, doubt that the United States was determined to save Southeast Asia and doubt that President Diem in South Vietnam had the capability to deal effectively with Communist methods. Taylor concluded that the outcome of the struggle in Vietnam depended largely on what the United States decided to do, or not do, and he strongly recommended to the President that the United States make a "broad commitment to a joint effort with Diem" to mobilize the resources of both the United States and South Vietnam to win the struggle against the Vietnamese Communists, including the introduction of American combat forces into South Vietnam. [15]

In a private message to President Kennedy, dated November 1, 1961, General Taylor spelled out his reasons for advocating the introduction of American combat troops to Vietnam, albeit on a limited scale: "there can be no action so convincing of U. S. seriousness of purpose and hence so reassuring to the people and Government of SVN and to our other friends and allies in SEA as the introduction of US forces into SVN. The views of indigenous and US officials consulted on our trip were unanimous on this point." General Taylor, like Lyndon Johnson earlier, was candid in pointing to the following risks in this decision:

14 "Report by Vice President Johnson on His Visit to Asian Countries," *Pentagon Papers*, p. 130.
15 "Taylor's Summary of Findings on His Mission to South Vietnam," *Pentagon Papers*, p. 144.

a. The strategic reserve of US forces is presently so weak that we can ill afford any detachment of forces to a peripheral area of the Communist bloc where they will be pinned down for an uncertain duration. b. Although US prestige is already engaged in SVN, it will become more so by the sending of troops. c. If the first contingent is not enough to accomplish the necessary results, it will be difficult to resist the pressure to reinforce. If the ultimate result sought is the closing of the frontiers and the clean-up of the insurgents within SVN, there is no limit to our possible commitment (unless we attack the source in Hanoi). d. The introduction of US forces may increase tensions and risk escalation into a major war in Asia.

Taylor concluded with the assertion that the introduction of a "military task force without delay offers definitely more advantage than it creates risks and difficulties" and concluded that "I do not believe that our program to save SVN will succeed without it."[16]

The report of the Taylor mission to Vietnam set in high gear the policy-making machinery of the government, culminating in a National Security Council meeting with the President in mid-November 1961. The key question to be decided by the President was: How important is Vietnam to United States national interests in Southeast Asia, and in Asia as a whole? A second and subordinate question was: What price is the United States willing to pay to prevent a Communist takeover in South Vietnam, assuming the answer to the first question was that South Vietnam should not be abandoned? Secretary of Defense Robert McNamara put the issues in sharp focus in a memorandum to the President dated November 8: "The basic issue framed by the Taylor Report is whether the U. S. shall: a. Commit itself to the clear objective of preventing the fall of South Vietnam to Communism, and b. Support this commitment by necessary immediate actions and preparations for possible later actions." McNamara reported that he and the Joint Chiefs of Staff and Deputy Secretary of Defense Roswell Gilpatric were in agreement that: "The fall of South Vietnam to Communism would lead to the fairly rapid extension of Communist control, or complete accommodation to Communism, in the rest of mainland Southeast Asia and in Indonesia. The strategic implications worldwide,

[16] "Cable from Taylor to Kennedy on Introduction of U.S. Troops," *Pentagon Papers*, pp. 141, 142.

particularly in the Orient, would be extremely serious." McNamara agreed with Taylor's gloomy assessment of stemming the tide in South Vietnam without the introduction of United States troops: "The chances are against, probably sharply against, preventing that fall by any measures short of the introduction of U. S. forces on a substantial scale." The Secretary of Defense did not feel that Hanoi would be dissuaded from pursuing its war of national liberation by token American forces, and "we would be almost certain to get increasingly mired down in an inconclusive struggle." He estimated that it would require up to six divisions of ground troops (about 205,000 men) to deal with a sustained Communist drive to take over South Vietnam. McNamara cautioned that "military force is not the only element of what must be a most carefully coordinated set of actions. Success will depend on factors many of which are not within our control – notably the conduct of Diem himself and other leaders in the area." He also warned that "the domestic political implications of accepting the objective [a full commitment to save Vietnam] are also grave, although it is our feeling that the country will respond better to a firm initial position than to courses of action that lead us in only gradually and that in the meantime are sure to involve casualties." He also believed that permitting South Vietnam to fall would strengthen and encourage Moscow and Peking in their policies. In sum, Secretary McNamara, speaking for the Joint Chiefs of Staff as well as himself, made these recommendations to the President:

a. We do not believe major units of U. S. forces should be introduced in South Vietnam unless we are willing to make an affirmative decision on the issue stated at the start of this memorandum [a full commitment to save South Vietnam]. b. We are inclined to recommend that we do commit the U. S. to the clear objective of preventing the fall of South Vietnam to Communism and that we support this commitment by the necessary military actions. c. If such a commitment is agreed upon, we support the recommendations of General Taylor as the first steps toward its fulfillment.[17]

Secretary of State Dean Rusk made his recommendations to the President in a memorandum dated November 11, 1961, and

[17] "Conclusion of McNamara on Report by General Taylor," *Pentagon Papers,* pp. 148, 149, 150.

his views were concurred in by McNamara.[18] Rusk addressed the question of United States national interests in South Vietnam in specific terms:

The deteriorating situation in South Viet-Nam requires attention to the nature and scope of United States national interests in that country. The loss of South Viet-Nam would make pointless any further discussion about a nation of 20 million people from the free world to the Communist bloc. The loss of South Viet-Nam would make pointless any further discussion about the importance of Southeast Asia to the free world; we would have to face the near certainty that the remainder of Southeast Asia and Indonesia would move to a complete accommodation with Communism, if not formal incorporation with the Communist bloc. The United States, as a member of SEATO, has commitments with respect to South Viet-Nam under the Protocol to the SEATO Treaty. . . . The loss of South Viet-Nam to Communism would not only destroy SEATO but would undermine the credibility of American commitments elsewhere. Further, loss of South Viet-Nam would stimulate bitter domestic controversies in the United States and would be seized upon by extreme elements to divide the country and harass the Administration.

After thus defining what he saw as the national interest in Vietnam, Rusk recommended that "We now take the decision to commit ourselves to the objective of preventing the fall of South Viet-Nam to Communism and that, in doing so, we recognize that the introduction of United States and other SEATO forces may be necessary to achieve this objective. (However, if it is necessary to commit outside forces to achieve the foregoing objective, our decision to introduce United States forces should not be contingent upon unanimous SEATO agreement thereto)." He concluded that the introduction of large military forces was not warranted at that time and that the major United States effort should be to bolster the capability of the South Vietnamese armed forces to deal more effectively with their own insurgency. However, both Rusk and McNamara were clear that large combat forces might have to be introduced if the South Vietnamese government of President Diem proved to be unable to stem the

[18] The Secretary of State, the Secretary of Defense, and the Vice President are statutory members of the National Security Council. The view of the Joint Chiefs of Staff are usually presented by the Chairman, who is always invited to attend council meetings when the possible deployment of United States forces is on the agenda.

rising tide of Communist insurgency without this kind of help.[19]

The importance of the *Pentagon Papers*, insofar as decision-making on military intervention in Vietnam is concerned, is the disclosure that the Kennedy administration as early as 1961 had come to the conclusion that South Vietnam was of critical importance to United States national interests in Asia and that its absorption into the so-called Communist bloc should be prevented by a major military effort if the South Vietnamese government could not stem the tide with its own forces aided by United States advisers and equipment. Even though President Kennedy decided against the introduction of American combat forces in 1961, it was clear in November of that year that the principal members of the National Security Council were agreed that South Vietnam constituted a vital national interest of the United States and had to be protected by United States armed forces if that became necessary. All the principal actors in this drama in 1961, with the exception of President Kennedy, were still in key positions in 1964–1965 when President Johnson had to make the final decision to send large combat forces to South Vietnam. They were: Secretaries Rusk and McNamara; General Taylor (then American Ambassador to Saigon); McGeorge Bundy, Assistant to the President for National Security Affairs; and Walt Rostow, Chairman of the State Department's Policy Planning Council. General Earle Wheeler had become Chairman of the Joint Chiefs of Staff in 1964, but he was no less dedicated than his predecessors to the view that if the United States abandoned South Vietnam, it must be prepared to abandon all Southeast Asia.

CRITERIA FOR DECIDING WHETHER VIETNAM WAS A VITAL INTEREST IN 1961

These memoranda and reports of key Kennedy administration officials in 1961 reveal a serious effort to analyze the pros and cons of a military commitment to save South Vietnam from a

[19] "1961 Rusk-McNamara Report to Kennedy on South Vietnam," *Pentagon Papers*, pp. 150, 151, 152.

North Vietnamese takeover. Contrary to popular belief, the documents show that the Kennedy and Johnson administrations did not blunder step by step into an expansive war in Southeast Asia but that they carefully weighed the costs, as they saw them, against the benefits they hoped to achieve by committing the United States to defend South Vietnam. Nevertheless, the question may rightly be asked: Did either the Kennedy or the Johnson administrations correctly assess the value of South Vietnam in terms of the total national interests of the United States? It is clear in retrospect that the key advisers of both presidents grossly underestimated the costs that eventually would have to be paid to prevent a North Vietnamese victory in South Vietnam; but, in my view, the more important question in determining whether South Vietnam was a vital interest of the United States was whether the intrinsic value of that country to the worldwide interests of the United States warranted the massive use of American military power there – a decision that apparently was made in the affirmative by President Kennedy late in 1961.

In Chapter 2 we discussed seven value faators that should be taken into account by policy-makers when they assess the degree of national interest the United States attaches to any foreign policy problem. These are: (1) location of the threat (geographic factor); (2) nature of the threat (open aggression or insurgency); (3) economic stake for the United States; (4) effect on balance of power; (5) effect on worldwide United States credibility and prestige; (6) support of major allies and the United Nations; and (7) historical sentiment of the American people. Let us examine the case of South Vietnam in 1961 against these factors and see whether the Kennedy administration correctly perceived the degree of national interest involved in Vietnam in 1961.[20]

1. *Location of the threat:* Few policy-makers or military strategists have ever argued that South Vietnam, or even the Indochina peninsula, constitutes a serious threat to the defense or security of the United States. Some have asserted that the United

---

[20] This is not to argue that these seven factors are the only ones which should be considered in determining the degree of national interest involved but that they constitute the most important factors which should be taken into account.

States' position as a Pacific power might be affected if South Vietnam were ruled by unfriendly leaders, but no one has sought to
equate the importance of Vietnam to such strategic areas as Cuba,
Iceland, Japan, or Canada – in terms of its importance to the
defense of the North American continent. In 1961, the United
States had no treaty with South Vietnam that obligated it to go
to war, although the SEATO treaty provided the legal framework for doing so in case the United States decided its national
interests warranted such action and South Vietnam requested
assistance. There were fewer than 1,000 American military personnel in Vietnam at the beginning of 1961, mostly advisers to
the Vietnamese army, and there was no implication that they
constituted a "trip-wire" similar to American troops in Berlin
or in South Korea. It could be argued, and was, that a Communist
takeover in Vietnam, Laos, or Cambodia would pose a critical
security problem for Thailand – which did have a defense treaty
with the United States through SEATO – and perhaps for the
Philippines, but this did not necessarily mean that United States
vital interests were at stake unless Thailand itself was attacked
by Communist forces across its borders. Therefore, on the basis
of location and strategic importance to United States defenses,
South Vietnam could not qualify as a vital interest of the United
States in 1961.

2. *Nature of the threat:* In 1961, there was no overt aggression
on the part of North Vietnam against the South, although there
was some infiltration of insurgents from the North and the supply
of equipment to the Viet Cong. No clear-cut invasion, such as
triggered President Truman's response in Korea in 1950, or like
the Soviet intervention in Czechoslovakia in 1968 (which did not
result in any military response from the United States) took
place in Vietnam. As General Taylor reported to President
Kennedy, the North Vietnamese effort in South Vietnam was
designed to bypass the conventional military forces in the area
and, by implication, to avoid triggering the provisions of the
SEATO treaty dealing with overt Communist aggression.[21] In so
doing, the threat in South Vietnam was considerably blurred,

21 "Taylor's Summary of Findings," *Pentagon Papers*, p. 144.

both for United States policy-makers, who had serious doubts about whether President Diem possessed the ability to mold a separate nation capable of withstanding the political appeal of the Viet Cong, and for the American public, which did not perceive any aggression in Vietnam that should cause the United States to go to war. To many thoughtful Americans, the Vietnam problem looked like a civil war without foreign intervention, and there appeared to be little reason for the United States to become involved militarily. Thus, on this score too, South Vietnam could not be viewed as a vital interest in 1961.

3. *Economic stake for the United States:* Here again, it was impossible to make any case that South Vietnam, or Indochina generally, was vital to American economic interests. There was practically no private American investment in the country and very little trade in 1961. In fact, South Vietnam, Laos, and Cambodia constituted a substantial drain on United States economic resources, even in this early period; Laos could not have survived as an independent state without the economic and military assistance provided by the United States, and South Vietnam probably could not have held together after 1954 without substantial aid to President Diem's government. Vietnam had no strategic materials, as did the Congo, for example, which might have given it a higher priority as an economic interest, nor did it constitute a potentially important source of raw materials, as did Indonesia. In fact, from a strictly economic standpoint, South Vietnam in 1961, as today, would have to be considered a negative factor in terms of United States national interests.

4. *Effect on balance of power:* It was on this point that the Kennedy administration advisers made their strongest case for considering South Vietnam a vital interest in 1961. It is clear from a reading of the memoranda quoted above that all the key officials – the Vice President, the Secretary of State, the Secretary of Defense, the Joint Chiefs of Staff, the Special Military Adviser to the President – thought that the adverse effects on the balance of power in East Asia resulting from a Communist victory in South Vietnam would be profound and that the United

States could not tolerate such a situation. Whether it was called the domino theory, which President Eisenhower had cited earlier, or some other concept to describe the importance of South Vietnam to the rest of Asia, it is clear from a reading of the *Pentagon Papers* that there was little doubt in the minds of key administration figures in 1961 that the stake was not just South Vietnam, but all Southeast Asia, including Indonesia (but probably not the Philippines). There was deep concern over the effect that Communist control over Southeast Asia would have on the future of United States relations with Japan and South Korea, as well as the boost such a victory would give to Chinese ambitions in Asia and to Soviet ambitions in other parts of the world. Vice President Johnson exaggerated somewhat when he said in his report to President Kennedy: "The basic decision in Southeast Asia is here. We must decide whether to help these countries to the best of our ability or throw in the towel in the area and pull back our defenses to San Francisco and a Fortress America concept."[22] His concern for the effect of a defeat in South Vietnam on the Asian balance of power was shared by all top advisers to President Kennedy in 1961.

There seems to have been little thought given by American government leaders in 1961 to the possibility that Thailand, or Malaysia/Singapore, or Indonesia might have continued a Western orientation in their foreign policies if South Vietnam were taken over by the Viet Cong. On the contrary, implicit in the view expressed by Kennedy advisers was the belief that all these countries would seek accommodation with the new political situation in Southeast Asia and make their peace with Hanoi and Peking. In the case of Indonesia, administration fears were substantiated when President Sukarno moved steadily toward accommodation with Peking from 1961 to 1965; in the cases of Thailand and Malaysia/Singapore, the assumption was not put to the test because their leaders responded favorably to President Kennedy's and President Johnson's decisions to defend South Vietnam. The key point here is that administration officials who were charged with assessing United States national interests in South Vietnam in 1961 perceived that country to be the plug in

[22] "Report by Vice President Johnson," *Pentagon Papers*, p. 129.

the tub of Southeast Asia; and although some of them may have had questions about the value of South Vietnam itself to American interests in Asia, particularly when they looked at the probable costs of trying to shore up the Diem regime against Viet Cong pressures, none of them was willing to write off Southeast Asia as a whole. Thus, the critical factor the Kennedy administration considered when deciding the degree of national interest implied in trying to save South Vietnam was not Vietnam itself, but rather the whole of Southeast Asia, and the effect that its shift of allegience would have on the future political course of such countries as Japan, India, and Indonesia.

5. *Effect on worldwide United States credibility and prestige:* Vice President Johnson, in the report cited above, said: "More important, we would say to the world in this case [abandoning South Vietnam] that we don't live up to treaties and don't stand by our friends." Or, as Secretary Rusk put it in his memorandum, also cited above: "The loss of South Viet-Nam to Communism would not only destroy SEATO but would undermine the credibility of American commitments elsewhere." Thus, prestige involves reassuring allies and friends that a great power will not abandon them when serious difficulties arise, or when costs go up. But perhaps even more important than reassuring allies is the necessity of deterring enemies from taking advantage of apparent weakness to press forward with risky adventures. In other words, how would Moscow and Peking in 1961 interpret a decision in Washington to withdraw from Vietnam? Would they give President Kennedy credit for showing good sense in pulling back from an untenable position, or would they interpret such a decision as a sign of weakness and indecision by the new President and use the occasion to test him further in other areas of the world, such as Berlin, Korea, or the Middle East? Secretary Rusk, during his eight years as Secretary of State, repeated this theme to the point of monotony to justify United States policies in Vietnam, and there is little doubt that every President since World War II has given a great amount of attention to this matter of "credibility of America's will" to protect its allies.

In 1961, American credibility and prestige seemed more important to President Kennedy than usual, for the following reasons: (1) despite the President's public warning to Moscow in March that the United States would act in Laos if the Pathet Lao drive toward the Mekong was not halted, he subsequently decided to negotiate for the *de facto* partition of Laos and a coalition government, which included the Pathets, rather than to send military forces there; (2) Kennedy suffered a serious loss of prestige in April over the Bay of Pigs episode in Cuba, where he permitted a covert operation to be launched and then failed to follow up with military force when the invasion of Cuba faltered; (3) Chairman Khrushchev had tried to intimidate the President in their June meeting at Vienna, and he subsequently erected the Berlin wall without any serious reaction from the United States. These three foreign-policy reverses during his first six months in office were on the minds of the President and his advisers, and the record indicates that in the fall of 1961 they were highly conscious of the need to make some show of will to impress on Soviet and Chinese leaders the Kennedy administration's determination not to be pressured into accepting any more diplomatic defeats by the Communist powers. Having decided against using force to preserve a pro-Western government in Laos, the next battleground in Southeast Asia was seen by Kennedy administration officials to be Vietnam, where the geography and the local situation were thought to be more favorable to a show of United States military power. The one large question mark in Vietnam was the ability of the Diem government to mobilize its population to withstand the Viet Cong and North Vietnamese pressure, and General Maxwell Taylor outlined in some detail the measures by which he thought this could be accomplished. Therefore, in 1961, the defense of South Vietnam was seen by President Kennedy as a test of will with the Communist Bloc, a struggle to regain prestige lost during the early months of the new administration. Vietnam became, then, the testing ground of whether a Western-oriented Asian country could cope with a war of national liberation. The stakes were high, because Kennedy concluded that if such a war could succeed in Vietnam, it could also succeed elsewhere in Asia and even in Latin America. Whether one can intellectualize prestige as a vital United States national interest is problematical; what is not in doubt is that American leaders in the fall of 1961 believed that American prestige in Asia was vital.

6. *Attitude of major allies and the United Nations:* Presidents Truman and Eisenhower had put much value on obtaining agreement from the British, and usually also from France and Germany (in Eisenhower's time) on a foreign-policy decision that involved the possible use of United States armed forces. Truman did so in the Berlin Crisis of 1948–1949 and in the Korean War; Eisenhower did so in 1954 during the Vietnam crisis and during the Lebanon crisis in 1958 as well as the several Taiwan Straits confrontations. However, it was apparent already in the late Eisenhower years that neither Britain nor France had much stomach for a confrontation between East and West over the mainland of Southeast Asia. France was bitter over Washington's failure to come to its support with military forces in Vietnam in 1954, as well as subsequent American efforts to ease out French advisers and influence there. Britain, which had military forces in Malaysia and Singapore and strong economic ties in the area, gave diplomatic support to United States policy on the mainland, but by 1961 Britain opposed SEATO intervention in Laos and favored instead negotiations with the Soviet Union and China to avoid war there. Britain also was not favorable to a military intervention in South Vietnam, in part because Britain's own experience in dealing with an insurgency in Malaya caused her to have serious doubts about whether South Vietnam had the political viability to withstand North Vietnamese pressures, even with substantial military support. Thus, two of America's principal SEATO allies were either opposed or lukewarm in 1961 to making a stand in South Vietnam. Two other, but much smaller, SEATO allies – Australia and New Zealand – were prepared to support an American effort in South Vietnam, but their contribution to the effort would always have to be considered marginal in terms of the military power they could bring to bear. Thailand and the Philippines, the only two Southeast Asian partners in SEATO, strongly favored military action to save South Vietnam, but again their contributions to such an effort could be considered marginal at best.[23] Japan took no public stand in favor of United States intervention in South Vietnam, even though one of the major factors influencing American policy-makers in 1961 was concern about the future position of Japan if Southeast Asia succumbed to Communist influence. The United Nations was never permitted by either side to take up the Vietnam problem.

President Kennedy, and after him President Johnson, had to decide whether to intervene militarily to save South Vietnam without the support of either of America's two most important postwar allies – Britain and France. Even though the United States government did not need large military forces from either country, it did need their political support in order to persuade the American people that Vietnam was a just cause for which to ask American men to risk their lives. Britain did give political but not military support to the United States build-up in Vietnam; France did not give either. Therefore, we may conclude that in 1961 the participation of major allies was not a key factor in the determination of whether South Vietnam was a vital United States interest.

7. *Historical sentiment of the American people:* It is important to distinguish here between public opinion, which is subject to rapid change depending on the specific issue and the context in which an opinion is asked, and the longer-term sentiments or attitudes of the American people toward foreign-policy matters. For example, American policy toward China in the 1940's was heavily influenced by the sentiments of many American people, developed over half a century of contacts with China, who perceived support for Chiang Kai-shek's China to be a very high priority on America's scale of interests. In the case of South Vietnam, no such attachment for the people or the country existed in 1961. Indochina was for nearly a century the colonial pre-

---

[23] U.S., Congress, Senate, Committee on Foreign Relations, *Hearings before the Subcommittee on United States Security Agreements and Commitments Abroad,* 91st Cong., 2d sess., 1970, showed that both Thailand and the Philippines received substantial amounts of aid in return for sending modest military forces to Vietnam. Australia and New Zealand, on the other hand, paid the entire cost of their forces in Vietnam.

serve of France, and unlike the Philippines – where the United States felt a moral obligation because of its colonial rule after 1899 – Vietnam was unknown to most Americans and, therefore, unloved. Other factors have influenced American public sentiments in favor of certain foreign countries in this century: Finland because it paid its World War I war debts, Czechoslovakia because it was a true democracy in a region traditionally dominated by authoritarian governments, and Korea because it was the object of a brutal aggression in 1950. These are factors that can arouse basic American sentiments in favor of certain foreign countries, but none of them was present in the case of South Vietnam in 1961. In fact, the authoritarian regime of President Diem was a negative factor in Washington's effort to obtain support for its commitment there, both among the American people and among America's democratic allies. Therefore, we may conclude that positive historical sentiment of the American people was completely lacking in the case of Vietnam. When President Kennedy had to make his crucial decision about using American power to save South Vietnam, he did so in the knowledge that if the effort proved to be costly and of long duration, he or his successor would probably be faced with serious opposition within the United States and in Congress over the wisdom of that decision.

Of these seven value factors, which should be taken into account when the United States decides whether a foreign-policy issue involves a vital national interest, only two could reasonably be answered in the affirmative by policy-makers concerned with the Vietnam problem in 1961, namely, the balance of power in the Far East and the effect on America's worldwide credibility and prestige. The question for historians to assess is whether these were sufficient reasons for the President to commit the United States to a large war on the continent of Asia. President Truman took the nation to war in Korea in 1950 because of a flagrant act of aggression, and he had both United Nations support and the active participation of America's key allies; yet, that war became unpopular with the American people because there appeared to be no direct threat to the United States. One may argue that once the United States accepted the role of great power and assumed worldwide responsibilities, the President had the duty to be constantly concerned about the world balance of power and the credibility of America's commitments to other countries. Consequently, it might be argued, President Kennedy could reasonably decide on the basis of these two factors alone that Vietnam was a vital United States interest and had to be protected with arms, if necessary. On the other hand, it can be argued that assessments about the impact of American actions on the world balance of power and on American credibility and prestige are not sharply drawn but must take into account the degree of risk the President is willing to take. In 1954 President Eisenhower was willing to accept certain risks regarding the balance of power and American prestige, which President Kennedy in 1961 apparently was not willing to do. Both knew that they would have little support in Congress or among the people for a long and costly war in Vietnam; yet, Kennedy viewed the issue as vital to the nation's interests whereas Eisenhower stopped short of committing United States forces. Therein lies an important variable in any assessment of national interests: the personality and perceptions of an individual man with great constitutional authority to make these assessments.

PERCEPTION OF INTERESTS BY THE JOHNSON ADMINISTRATION

The *Pentagon Papers* have brought to light the fact that the basic decisions about United States interests in Vietnam and its willingness to go to war to uphold those interests were reaffirmed by the Johnson administration in the spring of 1964, not in 1965 as many observers previously believed. The impetus for these decisions by the new President was a deteriorating political and security situation within South Vietnam, following the overthrow of the Diem regime in November 1963, and an assessment made by Secretary of Defense McNamara following a visit to Vietnam in December that "Current trends, unless reversed in the next 2–3 months, will lead to neutralization at best and more likely to a Communist-controlled state."[24] The Joint Chiefs of

---

[24] "McNamara Report to Johnson on the Situation in Saigon in '63," *Pentagon Papers*, p. 271.

Staff followed this gloomy report with a strong recommendation "that the United States must be prepared to put aside many of the self-imposed restrictions which now limit our efforts, and to undertake bolder actions which may embody greater risks." In a memo to McNamara dated January 22, 1964, General Maxwell Taylor, Chairman of the Joint Chiefs of Staff, stated: "The Joint Chiefs of Staff are increasingly mindful that our fortunes in South Vietnam are an accurate barometer of our fortunes in all of Southeast Asia. It is our view that if the U.S. program succeeds in South Vietnam it will go far toward stabilizing the total Southeast Asia situation. Conversely, a loss of South Vietnam to the communists will presage an early erosion of the remainder of our position in that subcontinent."[25]

On March 17, 1964, the White House issued a National Security Action Memorandum (NSAM) entitled "U.S. Objectives in South Vietnam." A NSAM always was issued with the approval of the President, usually following a meeting of the National Security Council, and provided guidance to all government agencies on presidential decisions. This particular NSAM was significant because it set forth in clear terms the new President's view of United States interests in Vietnam and set the stage for the military intervention that was to take place step by step during the following fifteen months. The document stated that it was United States policy to "prepare immediately to be in a position on 72 hours notice to initiate the full range of Laotian and Cambodian 'Border Control actions' . . . and the 'Retaliatory Actions' against North Vietnam, and to be in a position on 30 days' notice to initiate the program of 'Graduated Overt Military Pressure' against North Vietnam." The objective of United States policy was seen as an independent, non-Communist South Vietnam:

We do not require that it serve as a Western base or as a member of a Western Alliance. South Vietnam must be free, however, to accept outside assistance as required to maintain its security. . . . Unless we can achieve this objective in South Vietnam, almost all of Southeast Asia will probably fall under Communist domination (all of Vietnam, Laos, and Cambodia), accommodate to Communism so as to remove effective U.S. and anti-

---

[25] " '64 Memo by Joint Chiefs of Staff Discussion on Widening of the War," *Pentagon Papers*, p. 274.

Communist influence (Burma), or fall under the domination of forces not now explicitly Communist but likely then to become so (Indonesia taking over Malaysia). Thailand might hold for a period without help, but would be under grave pressure.

The document took account of the growing American involvement in Vietnam since 1954 and especially since 1961 and said that in the rest of the world the "South Vietnam conflict is regarded as a test case of U.S. capacity to help a nation to meet the Communist 'war of liberation.' Thus, purely in terms of foreign policy, the stakes are high." At another point, the document asserts, "In any case it is vital that we continue to take every reasonable measure to assure success in South Vietnam."[26]

In subsequent months of 1964, detailed planning went forward within the government to prepare for military intervention in Vietnam, first with air strikes against North Vietnam, increased covert operations in the North, greater military assistance to the South Vietnamese army, and the introduction of United States ground forces, if that became necessary. Planning also took place to obtain a resolution of support from Congress for military action in Vietnam, and the Tonkin Gulf Resolution was obtained in August following a North Vietnamese attack on United States naval vessels in the South China Sea. The *Pentagon Papers* show that President Johnson was reluctant at points to authorize specific military actions, probably because of the presidential elections of November 1964; however, the basic decisions about the importance of Vietnam and the necessity to fight, if necessary, had been taken almost a year before the sustained bombing of North Vietnam began in February 1965 and the subsequent introduction of ground forces into South Vietnam. In a memo dated March 24, 1965, on the eve of the sending of United States Army units to Vietnam, Assistant Secretary of Defense John Mc-Naughton, one of the key second-echelon advisers to the President on Vietnam policy, summarized for Secretary McNamara his view of why the United States was intervening militarily in Vietnam: 70 percent was in order "to avoid a humiliating U.S. defeat (to our reputation as a guarantor)"; another 20 percent

26 "U.S. Order for Preparations for Some Retaliatory Action," *Pentagon Papers*, pp. 283, 284.

was to prevent South Vietnam and nearby countries from falling into "Chinese hands"; and only 10 percent was to help the people of South Vietnam to enjoy "a better, freer way of life." McNaughton, who apparently had doubts about the efficacy of the United States effort, asked the following question: "Can the situation inside SVN be bottomed out (a) without extreme measures against the DRV and/or (b) without deployment of large numbers of U.S. (and other) combat troops inside SVN? The answer is perhaps, but probably no."[27]

President Johnson intervened in Vietnam, therefore, because he perceived, as did President Kennedy, that a Viet Cong–North Vietnamese victory in South Vietnam would probably result in the loss to Communist influence of most if not all Southeast Asia, and that the effect of this change on the Asian balance of power would be unacceptable to the United States. The second factor, as in 1961, was the effect of a defeat on United States worldwide credibility as an ally and the consequent blow to its prestige as a great power. These factors apparently were felt as strongly by President Johnson as they had been by John Kennedy. The difference was that in 1961 the political situation in South Vietnam was poor, but not desperate; by 1964 it was becoming desperate and armed intervention was seen as the only way to avoid a disastrous diplomatic defeat for the United States.

THE NIXON DOCTRINE AND VIETNAM

If the Kennedy and Johnson administrations proceeded on the assumption that saving South Vietnam was a vital national interest of the United States, the statements and actions of the Nixon administration seem to suggest that the United States no longer considers this to be so. In his 1971 report to Congress on foreign policy, President Nixon made the following statement about the United States' response to aggression that does not involve one of the nuclear powers: "We will continue to provide elements of military strength and economic resources appropriate to our size and our interests. But it is no longer natural or pos-

[27] "McNaughton Draft for McNamara on 'Proposed Course of Action,' " *Pentagon Papers*, pp. 432, 433.

sible in this age to argue that security or development around the globe is primarily America's concern. The defense and progress of other countries must be first their responsibility and second, a regional responsibility." In speaking of the need to reassess past policies, the President spoke specifically of Vietnam: "Others [vestiges of the past] must be liquidated, but the method is crucial. Clearly, we could not have continued the inherited policy on Vietnam. Just as clearly, the way in which we set about to resolve this problem has a major impact on our credibility abroad and our cohesion at home."[28] In discussing the reasons why he had decided on deescalation of the Vietnam conflict, the President said: "Some urged that we escalate in an attempt to impose a military solution on the battlefield. We ruled out this approach because of the nature of the conflict and of the enemy, the costs of such a policy, the risks of a wider war, and the deeply held convictions of many of our people."[29] In effect, Nixon was saying that the struggle in Vietnam was not vital to American interests in the world and that seeking a military solution to the war was not worth the costs involved. Therefore, a diplomatic solution which did not abandon South Vietnam was seen as the objective: "We sought above all a rapid negotiated solution to the conflict by progressively defining the terms of a settlement that would accommodate the legitimate interests of both sides. And in the absence of a settlement, we sought through Vietnamization, to shift American responsibilities to the South Vietnamese."[30]

President Nixon dramatized his new view of United States interests in Asia when he announced on July 15, 1971, that he had sent his assistant Henry Kissinger to Peking to confer with Chinese leaders and when he himself visited China in February 1972. The President justified this rather remarkable shift in United States policy and interests in the Far East with this statement: "As I have pointed out on a number of occasions over the past three years, there can be no stable and enduring peace without the participation of the People's Republic of China and its

28 *U.S. Foreign Policy for the 1970's: Building for Peace* (Washington, D.C., 1971), pp. 14, 15.
29 Ibid., p. 61.
30 Ibid., p. 65.

740 million people. That is why I have undertaken initiatives in several areas to open the door for more normal relations between our two countries. . . . I have taken this action because of my profound conviction that all nations will gain from a reduction of tensions and a better relationship between the United States and the People's Republic of China."[31]

Thus, within the span of only ten years, 1961–1971, the United States government's perception of its national interests in Asia underwent a dramatic shift. In the fall of 1961, the view in Washington was that China posed an ominous threat to American interests throughout East Asia, particularly in Southeast Asia, and that these interests were so important that they had to be defended with United States troops if South Vietnam proved incapable of protecting itself; yet in 1971, another President representing another political viewpoint decided that China was not currently a serious military threat to United States interests in Asia and that an accommodation with Peking that would facilitate a political solution in Vietnam was more important to the United States than continued confrontation in Indochina. This sharp change in the United States' perception of its national interests in Asia will be the subject of much research and speculation among scholars for many years, and the rapprochement between Washington and Peking may well constitute one of the most significant changes in international relations in the latter part of the twentieth century. A number of external factors played a part, including China's fears of the Soviet Union, the astonishing economic power of a resurgent Japan, and the change in the regional balance of power in Southeast Asia following the failure of Sukarno's policies in Indonesia and the rise to power there of the moderate Suharto. Yet, another important reason for the changed American perception of its national interests was the apparent success of its policy in Vietnam in preventing the military takeover of South Vietnam by the North while withdrawing half a million American military personnel between 1969 and 1972. Historians might claim that President Nixon had no choice about withdrawing American forces, in

31 *Washington Post*, July 16, 1971.

view of the strong sentiments of the American people that Vietnam was not a vital interest of the United States. However, at the conclusion of 1972, it appeared that the United States had succeeded in preserving an independent South Vietnam and that it could revert to the Eisenhower concept wherein the mainland of East Asia would be viewed as a major rather than a vital American interest.

7

The Shifting Balance of World Power and United States National Interests

THE LATTER HALF of 1971 and the first half of 1972 proved to be a period of momentous change in the United States' perception of its national interests and in its formulation of foreign policy. The most striking example of the "new look" in this changed perception of interests was President Nixon's announcement in July 1971 that Henry Kissinger, his Assistant for National Security Affairs, had concluded a secret visit to Peking and that the President himself would visit Mainland China early in 1972. This shift of policy toward Peking was followed in September by Washington's acquiescence in the admission of the People's Republic of China to the United Nations and its assumption of the Security Council seat previously held by the Republic of China on Taiwan. President Nixon made his much publicized visit to Peking in February 1972, where he conferred with Chinese leaders and reached agreement on a reduction of tensions in East Asia, including the peaceful resolution of the Taiwan question.

A second momentous change in the United States' perception of its national interests was the President's decision in August 1971 to suspend the convertibility of dollars into gold, his imposition of a 10 percent surtax on imports, and his decision to place wage and price controls on the economy. Taken together, these measures served notice on America's major trading partners – Japan, Canada, and the West European countries – that the United States no longer was willing to see its balance-of-payments account and its foreign-trade balance deteriorate because of the reluctance of other trading powers to revalue their currencies, as well as remove restrictions on the import of American goods and investments into their markets. Although the Smithsonian Agreements in December 1971 in Washington resulted in the devaluation of the dollar by 8 percent and the revaluation of several other currencies, this was seen as a temporary arrangement pending a thorough overhaul of the international monetary system necessitated by the United States' reappraisal of its international economic interests.

The third momentous event of this period was President Nixon's visit to Moscow in May 1972, where he concluded a Strategic Arms Limitation Agreement with Soviet leaders and set in motion a large sale of agricultural products to the U.S.S.R. The Soviet Union had previously concluded agreements with the Western Powers and with West Germany safeguarding western access to Berlin and gave the impression of genuinely seeking detente in Europe as its relations with Peking continued to be marked by hostility. The Moscow Summit clearly indicated that the superpowers wished to reduce tensions between them and to make progress on a limitation of armaments.

Finally, during this same period of July 1971–June 1972, the Nixon administration decided to support Pakistan against India when the latter sent its forces into East Pakistan and threatened West Pakistan as well. This action was not so dramatic as the others nor was it as well understood by the American public; but it was part of a pattern of actions taken by Nixon during 1971–1972 that could be explained under the heading of an old concept in international relations known as "balance-of-power politics."

In an interview with *Time* magazine at the end of 1971, President Nixon made the following significant statement about the world balance of power:

We must remember the only time in the history of the world that we have had any extended periods of peace is when there has been balance of power. It is when one nation becomes infinitely more powerful in relation to its potential competitor that the danger of war arises. So I believe in a world in which the United States is powerful. I think it will be a safer world and a better world if we have a strong, healthy United States, Europe, Soviet Union, China, Japan, each balancing the other, not playing one against the other, an even balance.[1]

In Nixon's view, the United States does not have to be supreme in world politics in order to feel safe; safety can be achieved through a balance of power in which no single nation, however powerful, believes that the benefits of warfare outweigh the risks and costs. This was a significant departure from the prevailing view in the 1950's and 1960's, which assumed that American supremacy was essential to world peace and security.

The President's visit to Peking represented the most dramatic evidence of movement toward a new balance of power as well as recognition that China does not pose the same military threat to United States interests in Asia that seemed true in the 1950's and early 1960's. In fact, closer relations with Peking could prove beneficial to the United States in its dealings with the Soviet Union and other Asian countries during the coming decade. The new economic policy toward Japan initiated in 1971 would not have been feasible without first improving relations with China; the lessened tensions between China and the United States also had the effect of making Vietnam less dangerous to world peace.

The Nixon administration's decision to force the world's leading trading nations to agree on new exchange rates and to liberalize policies toward United States exports was made both for domestic and foreign-policy reasons, but the net effect was to dramatize a serious deterioration in the United States' international economic position and the need for improvement in the balance of trade in order to avert an even more serious international crisis. The President's series of summit meetings with European and Japanese heads of government during 1971–1972 resulted in some efforts among the major trading countries to accommodate America's need to reverse the serious imbalance in its payments account, but the real significance of the talks was the recognition of a need to establish a new balance of world economic power, taking account of Japan's remarkable economic expansion and the growing power of the European Economic Community.

The decision in December 1971 to "tilt toward Pakistan" in

---

[1] January 3, 1972.

its confrontation with India, perhaps the most controversial of the three decisions, was seen by many observers as a belated effort of the Nixon administration to halt a serious erosion in the balance of forces in South Asia, resulting from the withdrawal of the British presence and the growing relationship between India and the U.S.S.R., capped by a treaty of friendship and cooperation between them in the summer of 1971. According to official documents leaked to the press in December 1971, the President acted as he did because American leaders became convinced that India planned to attack West Pakistan after completing the occupation of East Pakistan, an action that would have altered the power balance on the Indian subcontinent in favor of the U.S.S.R.

Taken together, these foreign-policy decisions signaled a growing appreciation by the United States government of a shift in the world power balance in which an economically united Europe, a dynamic Japan, and an increasingly powerful Soviet Union are increasing their influence relative to that of the United States, at a time when the mood of the American people and Congress is to do less in the world and more at home. This decline in the United States' willingness to accept the principal burden of defending nations around the world against foreign pressure is causing most other countries to reassess their own policies in order to adjust to this new international power relationship. Nowhere is this better illustrated than in Japan where great misgivings have developed over future United States economic and security policies and their implications for Japan's well-being.

THE ATTRIBUTES OF POWER IN WORLD AFFAIRS

The term *power* is used so widely in international relations and with so little precision about its meaning that it has become almost synonymous with military strength. However, world power consists of more than military power, as Japan has clearly demonstrated in recent years.[2] A better term to describe this

---

[2] For an excellent analysis of this point, see Seyom Brown, "The Changing Essence of Power," *Foreign Affairs*, (January, 1973), pp. 286–299.

attribute is *influence* in world affairs – the ability of one state to cause another to listen attentively to its views and to do something positive about them. If *influence* could be substituted for *power* to describe the importance of nations, it would enable one to measure types of influence other than strictly military power. For example, despite a clear superiority in military strength, the United States was not able to bring about a political solution to the Vietnam conflict. Unfortunately, political scientists, statesmen, and military leaders probably are stuck with the term *power* because such terms as *great influencers* probably are not acceptable.

It is also important to distinguish among different levels of power, or influence, which nations possess in terms of their ability to change the policies of other states. Three such levels are suggested here: medium power, major power, and superpower.

A *medium power* may be viewed as a state that has the ability to influence significantly the actions of other states in its immediate geographical area. Indonesia, for example, strongly influences its neighbors' policies even though it has a weak economy and maintains modest military forces. Sweden has considerable influence in Northern Europe, despite a small population, because of its military and industrial capability.

A *major power* usually is capable of influencing the decisions of some states that are not in its immediate geographical location or, in the case of large land masses such as the Soviet Union and China, because they border on many smaller states whose interests and policies are divergent. Britain and France are examples of major powers in this sense because they continue to command influence outside of Europe, principally through economic aid and investments in Africa and some parts of the Middle East. Japan also fits this category because it has great economic influence in many areas of the world.

A *superpower* is one that exercises both military and economic influence in many parts of the world and also possesses a credible nuclear deterrent against any other superpower. Such a state is also capable of guaranteeing the security of lesser powers against pressures from any other nuclear power. At present, only the

United States and the Soviet Union fit this category, even though some others have a limited nuclear capability.

An important factor distinguishing a major from a superpower is that a major power normally does not take unilateral military action against another state unless its own survival is at stake. Instead, it will seek assistance from another major or superpower to protect its interests when it is endangered. An example was the British and French cooperation with Israel against Egypt in 1956 during the Suez Crisis. In that case, all three were forced to pull back because the United States and the Soviet Union opposed the operation.

Another distinguishing characteristic of a major power is that it does not possess, nor aspire to possess, a large nuclear-strike capability against potential enemies. Instead, major powers today are more likely to concentrate on building up their economic strength as the principal means of exerting influence, rather than employing military strength. Germany and Japan fit this latter pattern, as do Britain and France, although the latter possess limited nuclear forces. A superpower, on the other hand, may act without allies if it chooses because it runs a far lower risk of military retaliation. Soviet actions in Czechoslovakia in 1968 and United States action in the Dominican Republic in 1965 are examples of unilateral military moves by superpowers.

The ingredients that make for power and influence in world affairs are both tangible and intangible, and scholars and statesmen do not always agree on their relative importance. However, it is useful to review briefly what are considered to be the main attributes of a state that aspires to major power status or influence in the world. The following seven factors are not necessarily in order of importance, but each should be present to some degree in a country that aspires to be a major power: (1) economic and technological strength; (2) modern military forces capable of offensive and defensive operations; (3) a large, industrious, and educated population; (4) favorable geographic location and climate; (5) access to natural resources; (6) stable political system; and (7) effective leadership. Population is a factor that limits the number of major powers. Some states, such as Sweden, Australia, and Canada, would qualify if their populations were of significant size. In today's world, a country should have a minimum of 50 million people in order to provide manpower for both the industrial sector and the military forces required to exert significant influence outside its own geographical area.

By this standard, one may conclude that only seven countries qualify as major and superpowers in the early 1970's: United States, Soviet Union, China, Japan, Britain, France, and Germany. One can argue that India, Italy, and Brazil ought to be in this category, but it is difficult to make a case that these states, although potentially major powers, have the capability today to influence significantly events outside their immediate geographical areas. India, as a result of events in December 1971, may seek this role in Asia, but it is unlikely to achieve it in the foreseeable future. As for China, it is today a major but not a superpower because of its deficiency in economic and technological strength and in large nuclear forces. Although China probably aspires to superpower status, it is problematical whether, or when, she will achieve it.

Another important factor in the new balance of power is that, in contrast to the situation that existed until about 1965 – when the United States had a clear superiority over the Soviet Union in nuclear weapons – today they are about equal in the military sphere. Furthermore, whereas the United States has limited the growth of its offensive nuclear delivery capability in recent years, the Soviet Union apparently has not been willing to limit production of certain types of nuclear weapons, leading some United States authorities to conclude before the SALT agreements in May 1972 that the Soviets were seeking a first-strike capability, i.e., the ability to destroy the United States' nuclear force before it can be launched against the U.S.S.R. One may conclude that there is now virtual nuclear equality between the two superpowers and that in military power they far exceed all their rivals and allies. In the economic sphere, Japan has achieved third place and may well surpass the Soviet Union in GNP in this decade, and a united Europe including Britain, France, and Germany will in all probability be a great economic power by 1980. Politically, however, these three nations will continue in the foreseeable future to act independently.

THE EMERGING NEW BALANCE OF POWER

The key question in international relations in 1972 was how these seven major and superpowers would interact in the future, in light of the United States' decline as preeminent world power and the emergence of Japan, China, Europe, and the U.S.S.R. as growing power centers. If one accepts the saying that in international politics great powers abhor a power vacuum, the question naturally arises: Who will try to exert greater influence in such places as Southeast Asia, the Indian Ocean, and the Middle East as the United States reduces its own influence? Ever since President Nixon first enunciated his new foreign-policy objectives on Guam in the summer of 1969, other nations have been adjusting to what they perceive to be a general retrenchment of the United States throughout the world. Even though the President has reiterated his intention to honor all United States treaty commitments and defend nations threatened by nuclear powers, many Asian states see the American withdrawal from Vietnam as a sign it has downgraded the importance of Southeast Asia to its national interests. The President's visit to Peking in February 1972 seemed to confirm this fear, even though no specific changes were made as a result of that visit.

The risk to the United States, or any major power, embarking on a policy of disengagement from any area where its role has been paramount lies in the likelihood that other rival powers will take advantage of this decline to enhance their own positions. As Britain withdrew from the Eastern Mediterranean in the early post–World War II period, for example, the question President Truman had to decide was whether the United States would take up the burden of keeping the peace there or let that role fall to the Soviet Union – the most likely contender for hegemony in that area. Similarly, the British withdrawal from South Asia in the late 1960's created another power vacuum in the Indian Ocean area. From the Soviet point of view, this offered a tempting opportunity to extend its own influence there, in cooperation with India, because there appeared to be little risk of a United States challenge in light of the strong sentiment in Congress against additional foreign entanglements.

In retrospect, one can point to similarities between the Soviet-supported Syrian invasion of Jordan in September 1970 and the Soviet-supported Indian invasion of East Pakistan in December 1971; both episodes may be viewed as probes designed to test America's willingness to tolerate a change in the balance of power in two separate but important parts of Asia. In Jordan, the question was whether a weak but friendly regime could be toppled and thus place Israel in greater jeopardy from its hostile neighbors; in Pakistan, the question was whether the dismemberment of that country could be accomplished without retaliation and thus make India supreme in South Asia and possibly the Indian Ocean as well. In each case, the Soviet Union stood to gain considerable influence had the probes proved successful; conversely, the United States would have suffered a considerable loss of influence elsewhere had it failed to support its friends in these instances. What made each case especially important was that it occurred while the United States was disengaging from Southeast Asia and talking about withdrawing forces also from Europe. Similar tests are likely to continue so long as other expansionist nations believe they will not be opposed militarily if they move against troublesome neighbors. Another way of viewing this is to ask whether lawlessness is likely to increase when there is no policeman in sight? In some parts of the world, the answer to that question, unfortunately, must be "yes."

An overriding factor that must be considered when assessing the emerging new balance of world power is that the United States and the Soviet Union will continue to be the only paramount nuclear powers in the world in the foreseeable future and will maintain a "balance of terror" between them. Even though the United States is reducing its conventional military forces substantially in several areas, the Nixon administration has strengthened the strategic forces in order to prevent the Soviet Union from gaining an advantage in nuclear striking power. The concern shown over Soviet intentions to acquire a possible first-strike capability over the United States was evidence that Washington is not likely to permit Moscow to gain such superiority and then blackmail the United States into political concessions. Flowing from this nuclear standoff is a mutual interest in preventing the emergence of additional nuclear powers that could threaten the vital interests of either superpower. The question of China's future nuclear capability thus is of great importance to both Washington and Moscow, particularly the latter because of its long border with China and the growing hostility between them over the last decade. For similar reasons, the Soviet Union and the United States will continue to have a mutual interest in avoiding confrontations between them – such as the Cuban Missile Crisis – unless the survival of either is at stake; yet, this caution may not apply to support for third countries that desire to change the balance of power in a specific geographic area, and such probing will continue.

Given these considerations, what is likely to emerge from the adjustments now taking place among the major and superpowers? In Europe, a new balance is being fashioned among the European countries that will enable the United States in time to withdraw most of its ground forces, perhaps by 1976. The European Economic Community, which was expanded to nine nations in 1973, is a powerful new economic factor in world affairs and may become a political power as well in the next decade. A united Europe that can deal with the rest of the world from a position of similar interests will be a powerful counterweight to the Soviet Union and Eastern Europe. A continued American nuclear umbrella over Europe will be necessary, however. Agreement between East and West Germany in 1971 over access routes to Berlin and a peace treaty between West Germany and the Soviet Union in 1972 open the way for a mutual reduction of forces in Europe by both the NATO nations and the Warsaw Pact states. Modest United States forces will continue to be required in West Europe to man nuclear arsenals, but the large combat units stationed there since the early 1950's will no longer be required as the Europeans become capable of balancing Soviet conventional forces.

In East Asia and the Pacific region, the Nixon Doctrine clearly seeks to disengage the United States militarily from the mainland of Southeast Asia and to build a new balance of power there that will reduce the risks of war and United States involvement. The United States has pledged to continue its nuclear protection of Japan and other Asian nations against intimidation by any nuclear power, but the United States' military role in Asia will emphasize naval and air power rather than ground forces. The central question is: How will the security of the small, weak states of Southeast Asia be maintained if the United States refuses to use its own ground forces to resist limited aggression — aggression that is neither nuclear nor involves a blatant use of force, as in Korea?

The Soviet Union has made overtures to the Asian countries for a mutual security arrangement that would include India as well as the countries of Southeast Asia. If the United States is no longer willing to be the protector of Southeast Asia, and if countries such as Thailand, Malaysia, and Singapore believe their greatest future security threat will come from the north, will they be willing to join the Soviet Union's new security pact as an alternative? Some observers believe that Japan, which built a substantial economic stake in Southeast Asia in the 1960's, will be forced to look at its security interests there if the United States disengages. On the other hand, there is an equally strong possibility that Japan will not take on any security role in Southeast Asia because of the continuing strong public sentiment within Japan against embarking on overseas defense commitments.

As for China, the third major power contending for influence in Asia, what are her intentions in the 1970's? Will she continue to support insurgencies in Thailand, Laos, and possibly Burma, or will she find it in her own national interest to reduce tensions in the area in order to keep others, including the Soviet Union, out? This is the crucial question for the future balance of power in East Asia, for, in a real sense, the Soviet Union has replaced the United States as the principal threat to China's national interests. The American withdrawal from the mainland of Asia will make it possible for Peking and Washington — the two implacable enemies of the 1950's and 1960's — to forge a basis for maintaining the security of Asia against an expanding and sometimes belligerent Soviet Union. This is the real significance of the Nixon visit to Peking in February 1972.

That leaves Japan, the fourth major Asian power and the most important economic factor there. Despite its disenchantment over President Nixon's new economic policy and his visit to China, Japan probably has such a deep stake in maintaining close relations with the United States that it will not trade these ties for a close relationship with the Soviet Union or China. Neither Communist power can offer Japan the economic and security benefits now provided by the United States. However, Japan can be expected to follow a more independent policy in dealing with Moscow and Peking, particularly in economic affairs. Japan will also assume a larger role in the economic and political affairs of both North and South Korea, its closest neighbors, in order to lessen tensions there and improve its own security.

Thus, a new balance of power is emerging in East Asia, one where the United States will play a lesser role and Japan and the People's Republic of China will play larger roles. Together, these three powers will find it in their common interest to prevent the Soviet Union from extending its own influence both in Southeast Asia and in Northeast Asia. This new balance will not come about quickly or easily, because of deep ideological and historical differences separating China, Japan, and the United States; but as their perceptions of national interests change in the 1970's, so will their appreciation of the necessity of building better relations increase, in order to avoid costly confrontations among them in which the Soviet Union would be the major gainer.

American leaders have voiced the opinion that the Middle East is the most explosive area of the world and that another conflict there might well involve the United States and the Soviet Union. The Arab-Israeli War of 1967, the Jordanian crisis of 1970, and the India-Pakistan conflict in 1971 are symptoms of a serious conflict of interests between the superpowers in this key part of the world, which contains much of the world's known oil reserves and the most direct transit routes between Europe and the Far East. For two centuries Britain maintained the security of this area, keeping out both Czarist Russia and other Western powers, but after World War II Britain relinquished its role and in 1971 finally withdrew completely from the Indian Ocean and the Persian Gulf, leaving only modest forces in Singapore. How will a new balance be arranged to provide security both in the Middle East and in South Asia for those countries who feel themselves threatened by large neighbors? The Soviet Union clearly covets a larger role in this area, just as the Czars did, but Soviet leaders have an even more important reason today for increasing their influence in South Asia – containment of China. The United States has been reluctant to assume the British policeman's role in the Indian Ocean, particularly in the wake of the Vietnam experience; yet, in December 1971, it was forced by balance-of-power considerations to do more than it probably wished when Indian troops moved against East Pakistan. If the Soviet Union is able to exploit tensions on the subcontinent to enhance its own presence in the Indian Ocean area, this could prove dangerous to the interests of Japan and Europe – which rely heavily on Middle East oil – and thus to the broader interests of the United States. In a word, the previous balance of power in South Asia and the Indian Ocean is in danger of being upset, and the United States by its actions in December 1971 was seeking to shore up the dike while trying to forge a new balance there. A similar situation exists in the Eastern Mediterranean, where the United Arab Republic moved dangerously close to complete reliance on the Soviet Union before ousting Soviet technicians in the summer of 1972. The Soviet naval and air presence in the Eastern Mediterranean is evidence that Moscow has cleverly exploited the Arab-Israeli conflict to enhance its own influence there at the expense of the United States.

The crucial question for American policy-makers in the mid-1970's is whether they are prepared to concede a larger role to the Soviet Union in the Middle East and in South Asia, or whether they will resist this pressure with military power if necessary. If it is the former and the Soviet Union becomes the dominant power in the Middle East, this will have a profound effect on all the other major powers – Japan because of oil, China because of rivalry with the U.S.S.R., and Europe because of oil and trade. Such a major concession to the Soviet Union could result in a dramatic shift in the world balance of power, not merely in the Middle East. On the other hand, if the United States decides to resist Soviet pressures in South Asia as well as the Middle East, this will require a greater military presence in the area, as well as greater political efforts to obtain support not only from other major powers but also from medium Asian powers as well. This course clearly suggests larger economic and military aid for such countries as Indonesia, Malaysia, Singapore, Pakistan, Iran, and the Persian Gulf states, as well as some countries in East Africa. It would clearly call for closer relations with China, which has a considerable stake in what happens on the Indian subcontinent. Iran, with Western backing, might well become the key nation in the Middle East power equation.

UNITED STATES VITAL INTERESTS IN THE 1970's

In the final analysis, the changes in American foreign policy now taking place reflect a changing perception of the United States vital interests in the 1970's. If one defines vital interests as those so important to the security and well-being of the nation that it will use force, if necessary, to protect them, it is clear that in this decade the United States will have fewer vital national interests at stake in the world than it did in the 1960's. This is because the value attached to defending some areas of the world is declining as the costs of exerting American influence worldwide are increasing. In assessing which foreign policy issues are likely to be perceived as vital national interests, we should look at the problem in terms of the value and cost factors outlined in Chapter 2.

If certain so-called crisis situations in the world are measured against these value and cost factors today, it is certain that some will not be perceived as vital. The Vietnam experience is not the whole reason; equally important is the growing awareness among Americans that new power centers have emerged in the world and offer the possibility of shared responsibility for maintaining a world order, in place of the nearly unilateral responsibility accepted by the United States during the 1960's. The other, less obvious, factor is a growing realization among the American leadership that Moscow presents a greater danger to United States national interests worldwide than does Peking — at least in the foreseeable future. Therefore, in defining what American vital interests are in the 1970's, the assessment of the value and cost factors mentioned above will be significantly affected by the new emphasis given to balance-of-power politics; ten years ago these factors were, to a large extent, assessed on the basis of a preponderance of American power and the attitudes which flowed from this position. Whether the United States would have continued the preponderance-of-power politics in the 1970's had it been successful in Indochina in the 1960's can only be speculated; what is more clear is that the Nixon emphasis on balance-of-power politics probably was an inevitable outgrowth of the miscalculation of costs involved in the Vietnam intervention, plus the marginal value that large segments of the American people attached to Indochina. It can also be argued that balance-of-power politics is a natural result of a reassessment of United States vital interests in the 1970's and a greater willingness to accept disorder and conflict in some parts of the world, risks that were not taken in the 1950's and 1960's when America exercised preeminent world power.

In light of all these factors, what might reasonably be said about the new perceptions of American vital interests in the coming decade? Where are the places and what are the crucial issues that will continue to be so important to the security and well-being of the nation that it must be prepared to defend them with armed force, if all other measures short of that fail? Although any such speculation is risky and must of necessity be subjective, the following represents what I believe to be the most reasonable assessment of where the United States vital interests lie in this decade, based on the criteria of values and costs cited above. The three basic national interests described in Chapter 1 will serve as the framework.

Vital defense interests: Few Americans will quarrel with the necessity of protecting the territorial integrity of the United States and Canada against foreign military threats, and this will continue to be a vital, even survival, national interest in the future. Unless the American people have a high degree of confidence about the nation's security from attack, it would be difficult for any President to pursue other interests, either domestic or foreign. What, then, are the principal external threats to the defense of the United States that will concern the President and Congress in the future?

Clearly, the possibility that Soviet nuclear weapons could be launched against United States territory is at least a vital defense interest for the nation, and the Congress has not been willing to overrule the President's judgment of what is needed in military equipment to provide a credible deterrent to Soviet nuclear power, or the means to limit the damage to the United States if a nuclear exchange should occur. That is why Congress has not substantially cut the President's requests for increased strategic capability, for to do so would risk denying the President the military tools he may need to maintain a meaningful deterrent capability against the growing Soviet nuclear power. However, negotiations with the Soviet Union to reduce the risks of nuclear war are also a vital defense interest of the United States, and the Strategic Arms Limitation agreements, which President Nixon concluded in Moscow in May 1972, are evidence that both sides consider such negotiations to be in their vital interests.

The future threat to American territory of a nuclear armed China similarly is a vital interest of the United States, even though China will not have an intercontinental delivery capability until later in this decade. The reason China must be put in this category, but not Britain and France (also nuclear powers), is that China's intentions toward the United States have in the past been hostile. However, in 1972 there was a warming of relations between Peking and Washington; among the reasons President Nixon gave for making his visit to China was that it was of great concern to him that a nation of 750 million people armed with nuclear weapons should not be on speaking terms with the United States. Conversely, if China's intentions in Asia should prove to be hostile to American interests, then it would be a vital defense interest to protect American territory against China's growing nuclear capability, just as it has against the Soviet nuclear threat. Similar considerations would apply to any other major power that had both the capability of attacking the United States and hostile intentions toward American vital interests.

Aside from a threat to its territory, however, America's vital defense interests also extend beyond its borders to include countries whose security is so important to the defense of North America that the United States probably would go to war to prevent them from being absorbed into the sphere of influence of another power having hostile intentions toward the United States. Britain, Western Europe, and probably Japan fall into this category because their absorption into a power bloc hostile to the United States' interests would cause a drastic shift in the world balance of power and seriously affect the United States' ability to defend its institutions. Closer to American territory are smaller states and territories whose security is considered vital to its defenses, including Iceland and Greenland in the north Atlantic, the Azores and Bahamas in the mid-Atlantic, and all the states bordering on the Caribbean. Because of the expansion of United States defenses into the Pacific in the post–World War II period, the Trust Territories of the Pacific probably should be considered a vital defense interest.

Nations and territories that lie outside this defense perimeter must be considered of lesser importance to the defense interests of the United States, although some would be perceived as vital in terms of American international (world-order) interests. Southeast Asia, the Middle East, and the eastern Mediterranean area are examples: they do not constitute vital defense interests, but they have been perceived by some postwar presidents as vital world-order interests. The important factor here is the physical defense of United States territory and institutions, and for that purpose it is not essential that the territory of nations located far from American shores be protected by American military force.

Vital economic interests: For twenty-five years after World War II, economic interests appeared to take second place, behind defense and world-order interests, in United States foreign-policy priorities. However, in 1971 the American balance of trade and the value of the dollar had deteriorated so seriously that the President was forced to take drastic action to reverse the trend. In so doing, he dramatized to the American people and to the world his view that vital economic interests were at stake, and he called for measures by other countries to help reverse the trend. In 1971, the United States' balance of trade showed a deficit for the first time in seventy-five years, adding to the problems the government faced as it sought to reduce expenditures abroad while still playing a major role in international affairs. If the American economy had continued in 1972 and thereafter to experience both inflation and large unemployment, there was a great danger that the government would not be able to deal effectively with either foreign or domestic problems facing the country in the 1970's. If that trend had continued, protectionist sentiment in Congress would have persuaded the President to abandon much of the progress that has been made since 1945 in expanding world trade and commerce, and isolationist sentiment could have forced the President to abandon many forward defense positions overseas, including Europe and Japan, in the name of economy. Thus, the promotion of American exports and a more realistic rate of exchange of the dollar with other currencies became a vital interest of the United States in 1971, and there is every reason to believe that economic interests will continue to receive a high priority from both executive and legislative branches of government in the future.

The specific countries that will in the future be considered vital to American economic interests overlap considerably with those cited above under vital defense interests; they are the European Economic Community (Britain, France, and Germany being the most important), Japan, Canada, Mexico, Venezuela and Brazil. These are countries that have major trade with the United States and have large American investments. Certain other countries might be included because they possess important raw materials or because they are large importers of American products. These might include Australia, the Philippines, the Congo, South Africa, Argentina, and Chile. Some countries might be classified as potentially important for United States economic interests, but they could not be viewed as vital today; they include Indonesia, India, Pakistan, Greece, and the larger countries of Africa, such as Nigeria. China and the Soviet Union might well be important trading partners of the United States if they are prepared to open their borders to normal commercial relations. If the detente policy the Nixon administration pursued at the beginning of the 1970's continues and the Communist states respond affirmatively as they did in 1972, it is possible that trade will become a more important tool of American foreign policy than military power. The large grain shipments to the U.S.S.R. in 1972 is an example.

Vital world-order interests: It is in this category that the United States government will find the greatest ambiguity in trying to decide what its vital interests are in the 1970's.[3] Unlike national defense, which is measured largely in strategic terms, and economic interests, which can be gauged in terms of GNP and balance of payments, international or world-order interests have more to do with the psychology and sentiments of the American people, and this is infinitely more difficult to quantify than national defense or economics. The nub of the problem is that it is difficult to convince the American electorate in the 1970's that something as nebulous as "world order" is so important to the well-being of the nation that they must be willing to send their sons overseas to uphold this order, especially when costly wars such as those in Korea and Vietnam do not seem to threaten United States territory or its economic position. Whereas most Americans in 1945 probably favored the idea of collective defense embodied in the United Nations Charter, a majority today probably is opposed to armed intervention outside the Western Hemisphere, particularly when the issue is not one of overt aggression.[4]

The implications of this new mood of the American people are that future presidents and policy-makers will be obliged to downgrade United States interests in some parts of the world and accept more risks than their predecessors did in dealing with leftist and Marxist governments, particularly if they come

[3] For a challenging argument against America's assuming vital world-order interests anywhere outside the Western Hemisphere in the future, see Robert Tucker, *A New Isolationism: Threat or Promise*, New York, 1972, especially chapters 4 and 5.

[4] This point was strongly made by Walter Lippmann in an interview with Ronald Steel early in 1973 (*Washington Post*, April 1, 1973, pp. C 1, 4). Lippmann argued that defense of the homeland (survival interest) is the only justification for military intervention. He admitted that U.S. intervention to save Europe in World War II was justified, however.

to power through constitutional means and pose no threat to United States defenses. The confiscation of American private property by foreign governments will not in itself be perceived as a threat to the nation's security. Chile is an example. However, the granting of military facilities to the Soviet Union in any area considered a vital defense interest would certainly result in strong United States action.

In view of the above, what are likely to be American interests in areas such as Southeast Asia and the Middle East in the 1970's, areas where vital defense and economic interests are not involved but where this country has strong moral obligations because of previous commitments and, in the case of Israel, sentimental ties?

Southeast Asia presents a continuing dilemma for United States policy-makers because even though most of them might agree that Southeast Asia, particularly the mainland, is not a vital interest of the United States, the fact is that American interests have grown there since 1965 as a result of United States intervention in Vietnam and the large military build-up in Thailand. These circumstances make it very difficult for any President or policy-maker to take a completely detached view of future interests in Southeast Asia. A similar dilemma exists with regard to American interests in Korea, Japan, Okinawa, and Germany: once the United States expends lives and national treasure to defeat an enemy, or to protect a friend, it becomes extremely difficult to reduce the degree of national interest even though the passage of time clearly suggests that such a reevaluation of interests is warranted. In a word, it is unrealistic for policy-makers to think, as some political candidates suggested in the election campaign of 1972, that it will be possible for the United States to "wash its hands" of Indochina or Southeast Asia in the future and adopt a posture of peripheral interest there.

Nevertheless, it is clearly an important United States interest to reduce the degree of its involvement in Southeast Asia in the future, even though this course will entail risks for some of the nations there and result in the adjustment of their foreign policies accordingly. In assessing future interests in this region, the policy-makers should separate Southeast Asia into two parts – one made up of mainland countries of North and South Vietnam, Laos, Cambodia, Thailand, and Burma, and the other consisting of insular nations of Malaysia (actually a peninsula), Singapore, Indonesia, and the Philippines.

On the mainland, the post-Vietnam War period probably will see the total withdrawal of United States military forces not only from Vietnam but eventually also from Thailand. Prior to 1964, the United States had only military advisers in Thailand and primarily military advisers in Vietnam. Thai and Vietnamese leaders have stated on many occasions that they do not wish to have United States forces stationed indefinitely on their soil, and it would be consistent with their own national interests to have the United States play a limited role in their defense if the external threat diminishes substantially in the post-Vietnam War period. The Nixon policy of rapprochement with China is of immense importance in this equation; for if China and the United States can agree that neither will support local wars in Southeast Asia, then the external danger to Thailand, South Vietnam, and other countries on the mainland will decline and permit them to devote much more of their energies to improving the conditions of their own peoples and, it is to be hoped, make them less susceptible to subversion and insurgency from across their borders. The large assumption made here is that in a post-Vietnam War period, Hanoi as well as Saigon will honor the agreement settling the conflict and stop seeking to unite the two Vietnams by force.

If the danger of external attack on the mainland Southeast Asian states is greatly reduced and American military power is withdrawn after the settlement in Vietnam, what are the prospects that these states will be able to cope with their internal insurgency problems, which probably will continue to some extent in all of them? And what should be the United States' national interest in supporting the anti-insurgency efforts? In my view, Thailand and South Vietnam probably now possess the capability to contain North Vietnamese-sponsored insurgencies on their soil without direct American involvement; however, they will continue to require American economic and some military assistance in order to continue this capability, and the United States should be prepared to give such assistance provided it does not imply the future use of its forces. The weak points on the mainland of Southeast Asia will continue to be Laos and Cambodia which are not, and probably will never be, capable of defending their own soil against insurgents. Their independence will depend primarily on the willingness of the great powers in Asia to enforce a settlement of the Vietnam conflict that will include Laos and Cambodia. It may be necessary in the future for South Vietnam and Thailand to assume part of the responsibility of protecting these two states; but this would not be a happy solution for the Cambodian and Laotian peoples.

Perhaps the most sensible longer-term solution to the security problems of the mainland Southeast Asian countries lies in some form of neutralization, guaranteed by international treaty and enforced by the great powers of Asia – including Japan, China, the United States, and, perhaps, the Soviet Union. This would require an understanding among them that the mainland will be off-limits to great power exploitation and a willingness among them to prevent any of the six states of that area from upsetting the balance by military force. Such an understanding can be worked out only if all the powers agree that Southeast Asia is not an area they will contest in the future; and perhaps the terrible toll of the Vietnam War can provide the incentive for moving in this direction in the years ahead.

As for the nonmainland countries of Southeast Asia, it may be more difficult for them to remain aloof from great power entanglements because of the strategic location of Malaysia and Singapore, the size and economic resources of Indonesia, and the historical and sentimental ties of the Philippines to the United States. A new regional security system may eventually develop among these states that will avoid any entanglements with the great powers; but this is some distance in the future because of the basic weakness of all the states that might be included. Indonesia is undoubtedly the key to this relationship, and it seems likely in the mid-1970's that Indonesia will continue for some time to need the support of Australia, Japan, and the United States to achieve a power position from which it can eventually assert real leadership in insular Southeast Asia. Here the Soviet Union may try to play an independent role, as part of a larger design to increase its influence in the Indian Ocean area. That possibility will require the other powers, particularly the United States, to keep naval and air forces in the Western Pacific and to continue economic and military aid to Indonesia and the Philippines, and perhaps also to Singapore and Malaysia. However, Japan will probably increase its own aid there – if not naval forces – as its own national interests expand. But the important factor in future United States interests in this area is that it probably will not consider its own interests so deeply affected that it will be prepared to intervene with ground forces again. The American people will not be persuaded again that vital interests of any kind are at stake in Southeast Asia.

In the Middle East, one finds many parallels with Southeast Asia insofar as perception of United States national interests are concerned. The United States has no vital defense interests there, nor vital economic interests – although the growing need for Middle East oil may change this in the next decade. But it may well have vital world-order interests there because of moral commitments to the state of Israel and because of a desire to prevent Soviet control over the oil resources of the Middle East. Since World War II, five Presidents have stated that they would not stand by and permit other states to destroy the independence of Israel, despite the fact that the United States has no treaty commitment to that state. On several occasions – Lebanon in 1958 and Jordan in 1970 – the United States has taken military actions that showed its determination not to permit a shift of the balance of power in the Middle East. The United States government's announcement in January 1972 that it had negotiated a base agreement with Greece to permit the home-porting there of elements of the Sixth Fleet was a clear signal that the Nixon administration has no intention of abandoning its role in the Eastern Mediterranean, in view of the Soviet navy's expanded presence in that area. Critics argue that the United States has alienated the Arab countries and opened the way to Soviet penetration of the Middle East by supporting Israel so strongly against its neighbors. And this raises a crucial question for American leaders in the future: will their perception of a vital world-order interest in the Middle East be supported by the American public if the time comes when United States manpower and resources are needed to hold the balance of power there? In light of the Vietnam experience, the answer to this question is by no means certain, and American policy-makers no doubt hope that the Israelis will continue to be able to deal with any local conflict without direct American intervention. Therefore, it will continue to be in the United States' interest – probably a vital interest – to bring about an accommodation between Israel and its neighbors so that the United States may avoid the use of force to defend Israel against hostile Arab neighbors. In the 1970's, any president would risk repudiation at home if he took the nation to war in the Middle East.[5]

In light of the Vietnam experience, America's world-order interests will be decided to a much greater extent than before by a pragmatic approach to the relationship between costs and benefits in supporting countries that are of neither vital defense nor vital economic interest to the United States. In addition, future presidents will not have the same freedom as postwar presidents in making these assessments of costs and benefits because Congress and various interest groups within the country will insist on a major voice in determining national interests and in influencing the policies supporting those interests. Therefore, the challenge to the presidency is to formulate the United States' international interests in such a way that they will both protect the defense and economic interests of the nation in a rapidly changing international environment and at the same time win the support of a majority of the American people. It is probably too much to expect a new era of bipartisanship to emerge in the 1970's because of the agony over foreign policy in the 1960's, but it may not be unrealistic to think that nonpartisanship may be attainable on the broad questions of American international interests. If a new consensus can be built around the kind of role America should play in the world, to replace its preeminent role in the postwar era, it may yet be possible for the United States to celebrate its two hundredth birthday at peace with itself.

5 Walter Lippmann (op. cit.) answered the question as follows: "I don't believe that the intervention of American troops in Israel is desirable. I believe it would split the country and would go beyond the margin of a likely kind of war that Americans would fight as a patriotic war."

EPILOGUE

THIS STUDY of United States national interests in the 1970's would not be complete without taking note of two important developments early in 1973 that underscored the significance of earlier events and suggested an even tougher stand by President Nixon in defending American interests abroad than was apparent in his first administration. These were: (1) the way in which American involvement in the Vietnam War was finally ended, and (2) Washington's pressure on its major trading partners to adopt further currency realignments and trade policies favorable to the United States.

In Vietnam, a negotiated settlement was finally reached, recognizing South Vietnam's right to self-determination and implicitly rejecting the use of force by either side to achieve unification of the two Vietnams. Of major significance was Hanoi's failure to achieve what it had demanded for years – the ouster of the Thieu regime and its replacement with a coalition government favorable to Hanoi's objectives.

But the end of United States participation in the Vietnam struggle and the return of American prisoners of war were not achieved without another confrontation between the President and Congress over presidential powers in using the armed forces outside the United States and in determining the degree of national interest involved in a specific international crisis. In December 1972, President Nixon had decided to order B-52 bombers to bomb military targets in Hanoi and Haiphong, targets not previously hit because they were near heavily populated areas. He did this, according to his assistant Henry Kissinger, to force Hanoi to negotiate in earnest about the release of American prisoners of war in return for the withdrawal of all American forces from Vietnam, and not as a condition for a political settlement in South Vietnam. This action was perceived as an enormous risk by many members of Congress and many opinion leaders in the United States; they believed the President's dramatic action might enlarge the war at a time when it seemed to be ending, and some thought it might mean that American prisoners would never be released by Hanoi. The action carried large political risks for the President within the United States because the American people had been led to believe that peace was "at hand."

Had not a settlement been reached and the bombing halted by the time Congress reconvened early in January 1973, Congress very possibly would have cut off all funds for the war and might even have voted to censure the President. Even though this confrontation did not materialize – because Hanoi bowed to the President's pressure and agreed to release the American prisoners without further conditions – the emotions generated in the United States by the renewed bombing led to new congressional efforts to curb the President's powers to use the armed forces without a declaration of war. The lines were sharply drawn: the President believed so strongly in December 1972 that his view of how to end the war was better than that proposed by his critics in Congress that he decided to ignore them and send the B-52's over Hanoi. As a result of this action, many members of Congress believed so strongly that it must limit the President's authority that they renewed their efforts to pass legislation requiring the Chief Executive to get specific approval from Congress to use the armed forces in hostilities for more than thirty days.

The basis for the almost hysterical fears expressed by some political leaders and some segments of the press in December 1972, that the country was becoming a dictatorship, was that they perceived the President as flagrantly flouting the will of Congress and the American people. But the President probably had a large proportion of the American people behind him on the question of forcing Hanoi to stop "stalling" on the release of American prisoners, as Dr. Kissinger asserted its representatives were doing in Paris before the bombing was renewed. On the other hand, if the bombing had resulted in a larger war instead of a cease fire, it is likely that public sentiment would have turned against the President and Congress would have acted to cut off funding for Vietnam. Then the issue would have been a constitutional rather than a political one. As it turned out, the President won a great political victory over his opponents and was able to assert to the

American people, as he started his second term, that he had achieved "peace with honor" in Vietnam – although communist forces in Laos, Cambodia and parts of South Vietnam – bolstered by North Vietnamese cadres – continued their offensives against government forces after the ceasefire was proclaimed.

The Vietnam War, particularly the way in which it ended for the United States, underscored a fundamental issue in the relationships between Congress and the President and between the President and opinion leaders in the United States. This is the charge made by some government leaders that the Vietnam War would have ended sooner if Congress and the opinion leaders had not challenged Presidents Johnson's and Nixon's handling of the war and peace negotiations, thus giving Hanoi the expectation that America would eventually tire of the war and settle on Hanoi's terms. If one subscribes to the view that Hanoi was given "aid and comfort" by the protest marches and congressional criticism of the President's handling of the war, it is a small step to insist that such criticism should have been squelched by the government – at least the public demonstrations and the large publicity given to them. Such a view clearly favors government interference in the people's right of assembly and free speech during a time when Congress has not formally declared war. On the other hand, if one contends that the President should not have sent troops into Cambodia in 1970, mined Haiphong Harbor in May 1972, or used B-52's against Hanoi in December 1972, it can in turn be argued that more American troops would have lost their lives, the war might have continued indefinitely, and the American prisoners of war might still be held as hostages by North Vietnam.

What is important here is that the American system of government provides for a trade-off between great freedom of expression and dissent about the course and conduct of American foreign policy (greater, indeed, than in most Western countries) and centralized executive power to act when the vital national interests of the country are at stake. The dilemma is who decides when the vital national interests are at stake; and the President clearly has been given that authority by Congress since World War II. Whether Congress will retrieve some of that authority, and whether it should retrieve it, ultimately will be decided by the American people at the polls. But it may well be that the price the United States will continue to pay for protecting the great freedoms it provides its people to protest the President's perception of vital national interests is an acceptance of the Chief Executive's right to decide the intensity of interest when foreign policy crises arise.

President Nixon's economic moves in early 1973 underlined once more the significant shift that was taking place in the United States' perception of its national economic interests and the implications for the future of the international monetary system, which had been stable so long as the dollar was the international currency and the United States was willing to support it with gold. In early 1973, that was no longer true, and the specter of economic nationalism was beginning to appear on the horizon of international relations. The threat arose because each major trading nation is heavily influenced by domestic politics in its approach to the world's economic relationships.

The second devaluation by the United States in a brief time span and the continued pressure on the dollar in European money markets dramatized the fact that United States economic interests will be given far greater attention by Washington in the future than world-order interests. The continuing international monetary crises will probably push United States trade and monetary relationships toward the vital interest category, particularly with the ending of American military involvement in Indochina.[1] And as the public becomes more aware of the added challenge from abroad to the American economy, there will be increased domestic pressures for protection against foreign goods that displace domestic products. The serious nature of United States economic interest abroad will become even more apparent to the American people when nearly half of their oil supplies are imported from foreign sources in the next decade.

[1] Presidential aide Henry Kissinger's call at the end of April for the European Common Market nations to enter into a new "Atlantic Charter" with the United States appeared to many observers as an effort by the Nixon Administration to force Europe to make trade concessions to the United States in return for a continued United States military presence in Europe in the 1970's. Such "linkage" policies clearly suggest that the American government is giving economic relationships with Europe a higher priority than at any time since World War II.

With the ending of the Vietnam involvement and the growing awareness of America's relative decline as an economic power, it is predictable that the American people will look increasingly inward on their own domestic problems and pay less attention to the world. The worrisome question to world leaders, and to thoughtful Americans, is whether this new mood of turning inward and drawing the lines of vital national interests closer to American borders will result in Washington's taking too little responsibility for what happens in the rest of the world. It is a short step from the Nixon Doctrine of telling allies and friends to do more to help themselves before asking the United States for help to the next stage of saying that the United States really cannot do much to change many situations abroad, so why make the effort? This is the mood of isolationism, and it is likely to grow in the coming years if it is not checked by wise leadership in the White House and a high order of statesmanship in Congress. President Nixon has talked on many occasions about a "generation of peace," and in the early months of 1973 he could point to some notable achievements along the road to that goal. But the building of a stable world order – a peaceful international environment – requires real patience and perseverence, attributes which Americans have not traditionally been noted for.

This final look at where America is going in the world of the 1970's ends, therefore, on a cautiously optimistic note, trusting that the American people – particularly the post-World War II generation – will not turn their backs on the world as they seek to find a more realistic definition of United States national interests. For a peaceful international environment is essential both to the security and economic well-being of the United States, and such an environment cannot be built or maintained without the active participation of this country.

INDEX